Learned Helplessness, Welfare, and the Poverty Cycle

DISCARD

Other Books in the Current Controversies Series

Current
CONTROVERSIES

Learned Helplessness, Welfare, and the Poverty Cycle

Kristina Lyn Heitkamp, Book Editor

GREENHAVEN
PUBLISHING

Published in 2019 by Greenhaven Publishing, LLC
353 3rd Avenue, Suite 255, New York, NY 10010

Library of Congress Cataloging-in-Publication Data

Names: Heitkamp, Kristina Lyn, editor.
Title: Learned helplessness, welfare, and the poverty cycle / Kristina Lyn
  Heitkamp, book editor.
Description: New York : Greenhaven Publishing, [2019] | Series: Current
  controversies | Audience: Grade 9 to 12. | Includes bibliographical
  references and index.
Identifiers: LCCN 2018024583| ISBN 9781534503885 (library bound) | ISBN
  9781534504639 (pbk.)
Subjects: LCSH: Public welfare—United States—Juvenile literature. | United
  States—Social policy—Juvenile literature. | Poverty—United
  States—Juvenile literature.
Classification: LCC HV91 .L3534 2019 | DDC 362.50973—dc23
LC record available at https://lccn.loc.gov/2018024583

Manufactured in the United States of America

Website: http://greenhavenpublishing.com

Contents

Chapter 1: Should the Government End Welfare Entitlements?

John Wihbey

Stanford University investigated poverty and inequality in the United States by looking at economic data coupled with academic research to present an analysis of the nation's economic health.

Yes: Welfare Entitlements Create a Culture of Dependency

Arthur C. Brooks

Government aid programs that are meant to catch those who fall on hard times instead entrap them into a cycle of dependency, and children of poor families are hit the hardest.

Caroline Polk

Education is the most effective path to economic independence. However, government welfare entitlement programs stress work instead of educational goals.

Michael Tanner and Tad DeHaven

Private aid organizations can offer more flexible and diverse assistance to poor Americans, and without the expensive mess of paperwork and bureaucracy.

No: Word-Gap Is Just a Band-Aid on a Much Bigger Problem

Chapter 3: Is Poverty More Closely Related to Behavior than Economics?

Yes: Money Lessens Poverty, but Does Nothing to Change Behavior

No: Bad Behaviors Are a Result of Poverty, Not a Cause of Poverty

Chapter 4: Will Overcoming Learned Helplessness End the Culture of Poverty?

Yes: Overcoming Learned Helplessness Can Empower and Motivate the Poor

No: Poverty Is Not a State of Mind or a Choice

To break the cycle of poverty and crime, we must first evaluate the history and current conditions of impoverished neighborhoods. Growing up exposed to crime and with inferior education creates little hope for opportunities, and the priority should be on addressing these factors.

Chris Velasco

Social programs that are supposed to help people out of poverty are underfunded and spread too thin. Basic needs such as water, food, and shelter can't be provided by our government's safety net. The material reality of poverty must be addressed in order to combat it.

Foreword

*C*ontroversy is a word that has an undeniably unpleasant connotation. It carries a definite negative charge. Controversy can spoil family gatherings, spread a chill around classroom and campus discussion, inflame public discourse, open raw civic wounds, and lead to the ouster of public officials. We often feel that controversy is almost akin to bad manners, a rude and shocking eruption of that which must not be spoken or thought of in polite, tightly guarded society. To avoid controversy, to quell controversy, is often seen as a public good, a victory for etiquette, perhaps even a moral or ethical imperative.

Yet the studious, deliberate avoidance of controversy is also a whitewashing, a denial, a death threat to democracy. It is a false sterilizing and sanitizing and superficial ordering of the messy, ragged, chaotic, at times ugly processes by which a healthy democracy identifies and confronts challenges, engages in passionate debate about appropriate approaches and solutions, and arrives at something like a consensus and a broadly accepted and supported way forward. Controversy is the megaphone, the speaker's corner, the public square through which the citizenry finds and uses its voice. Controversy is the life's blood of our democracy and absolutely essential to the vibrant health of our society.

Our present age is certainly no stranger to controversy. We are consumed by fierce debates about technology, privacy, political correctness, poverty, violence, crime and policing, guns, immigration, civil and human rights, terrorism, militarism, environmental protection, and gender and racial equality. Loudly competing voices are raised every day, shouting opposing opinions, putting forth competing agendas, and summoning starkly different visions of a utopian or dystopian future. Often these voices attempt to shout the others down; there is precious little listening and considering among the cacophonous din. Yet listening and considering, too, are essential to the health of a democracy. If controversy is democracy's lusty lifeblood, respectful listening and careful thought are its higher faculties, its brain, its conscience.

Current Controversies does not shy away from or attempt to hush the loudly competing voices. It seeks to provide readers with as wide and representative as possible a range of articulate voices on any given controversy of the day, separates each one out to allow it to be heard clearly and fairly, and encourages careful listening to each of these well-crafted, thoughtfully expressed opinions, supplied by some of today's leading academics, thinkers, analysts, politicians, policy makers, economists, activists, change agents, and advocates. Only after listening to a wide range of opinions on an issue, evaluating the strengths and weaknesses of each argument, assessing how well the facts and available evidence mesh with the stated opinions and conclusions, and thoughtfully and critically examining one's own beliefs and conscience can the reader begin to arrive at his or her own conclusions and articulate his or her own stance on the spotlighted controversy.

This process is facilitated and supported in each Current Controversies volume by an introduction and chapter overviews that provide readers with the essential context they need to begin engaging with the spotlighted controversies, with the debates surrounding them, and with their own perhaps shifting or nascent opinions on them. Chapters are organized around several key questions that are answered with diverse opinions representing all points on the political spectrum. In its content, organization, and methodology, readers are encouraged to determine the authors' point of view and purpose, interrogate and analyze the various arguments and their rhetoric and structure, evaluate the arguments' strengths and weaknesses, test their claims against available facts and evidence, judge the validity of the reasoning, and bring into clearer, sharper focus the reader's own beliefs and conclusions and how they may differ from or align with those in the collection or those of classmates.

Research has shown that reading comprehension skills improve dramatically when students are provided with compelling, intriguing, and relevant "discussable" texts. The subject matter of these collections could not be more compelling, intriguing, or urgently relevant to today's students and the world they are poised to inherit. The anthologized articles also provide the basis for stimulating, lively, and passionate classroom debates. Students who are compelled to anticipate objections to their own argument and identify the flaws in those of an opponent read more carefully, think more critically, and steep themselves in relevant context, facts, and information more thoroughly. In short, using discussable text of the kind provided by every single volume in the Current Controversies series encourages close reading, facilitates reading comprehension, fosters research, strengthens critical thinking, and greatly enlivens and energizes classroom discussion and participation. The entire learning process is deepened, extended, and strengthened.

If we are to foster a knowledgeable, responsible, active, and engaged citizenry, we must provide readers with the intellectual, interpretive, and critical-thinking tools and experience necessary to make sense of the world around them and of the all-important debates and arguments that inform it. We must encourage them not to run away from or attempt to quell controversy but to embrace it in a responsible, conscientious, and thoughtful way, to sharpen and strengthen their own informed opinions by listening to and critically analyzing those of others. This series encourages respectful engagement with and analysis of current controversies and competing opinions and fosters a resulting increase in the strength and rigor of one's own opinions and stances. As such, it helps readers assume their rightful place in the public square and provides them with the skills necessary to uphold their awesome responsibility—guaranteeing the continued and future health of a vital, vibrant, and free democracy.

Introduction

> *A host of positive psychological changes inevitably will result from widespread economic security. The dignity of the individual will flourish when the decisions concerning his life are in his own hands, when he has the assurance that his income is stable and certain, and when he knows that he has the means to seek self-improvement.*[1]
>
> -Dr. Martin Luther King

According to the 2016 US Census Bureau report, approximately 40.6 million people in the United States participated in government assistance programs each month, including Medicaid and housing assistance. The poverty rate for children under age eighteen was 18 percent.[2] That is a lot of hungry mouths. However, the problem of poverty is certainly not a new issue. Poverty is a universal and tireless problem. America is one of the richest countries in the world, yet millions are living in poverty.

Before federal aid programs, aiding impoverished individuals was left in the hands of private charitable organizations. During the Great Depression of the 1930s, state and private charities were the ones setting up stations on the streets, serving food to the hungry. But their means were stretched too thin, and the welfare of families and children in poverty became a federal government responsibility. Shortly after entering office, former President Franklin D. Roosevelt (FDR) proposed and signed the Federal Emergency Relief Act that offered immediate relief. But FDR didn't stop there. The Roosevelt administration knew that fundamental reform was needed. The Social Security Act of 1935 provided elderly, physically challenged, maternal, and child welfare. [3] Although FDR knew the importance of providing for the poor, he thought that it couldn't be a permanent solution:

> A large proportion of these unemployed and their dependents have been forced on the relief rolls. The burden on the Federal Government has grown with great rapidity. We have here a human as well as an economic problem. When humane considerations are concerned, Americans give them precedence. The lessons of history, confirmed by the evidence immediately before me, show conclusively that continued dependence upon relief induces a spiritual and moral disintegration fundamentally destructive to the national fiber. To dole out relief in this way is to administer a narcotic, a subtle destroyer of the human spirit. It is inimical to the dictates of sound policy. It is in violation of the traditions of America. Work must be found for able-bodied but destitute workers. The federal Government must and shall quit this business of relief. [4]

Current critics of government-funded aid believe that these programs create a culture of dependency and entitlement. Speaker of the House of Representatives Paul Ryan wants to lift people out of poverty and onto a ladder of opportunity. He says that federal aid programs are failing and only making the situation worse. "We have a welfare system that's trapping people in poverty and effectively paying people not to work," Ryan said on a talk radio show.[5] Ryan believes the way out of the mess is to cut funding for welfare programs, such as Medicare, Medicaid, and food stamps. Plus, he highlights the added bonus of slashing funding: it will help reduce the federal deficit.

Some critics of government welfare claim that it's time to pass the torch back to private charity. They argue that private charitable organizations are better at handling the diversity of needs created by poverty. One of the most successful businessmen and philanthropists agrees. Every year, Bill and Melinda Gates offer an annual letter that discusses their philanthropic work, lessons learned, and goals for the future. In their 2018 annual letter, Bill Gates touts the potential of the private sector in brainstorming solutions to the complex issue of poverty:

> We think poor people should benefit from the same kind of innovation in health and agriculture that has improved life in the richest parts of the world. Much of that innovation comes out of the private sector. But companies have to make a return on their investments, which means they have little incentive to work on problems that mainly affect the world's poorest people. We're trying to change that—to encourage companies to focus a bit of their expertise on the problems of the poor without asking them to lose money along the way. [6]

Despite criticism, advocates for social welfare programs note that in recent years the official poverty rate has fallen and the median income levels have increased. The 2016 US Census Bureau report also highlighted that the official poverty rate was down, with 2.5 million fewer people living in poverty than the year before. Programs that approach breaking the poverty cycle from a different angle, such as public action campaigns that promote bridging the word gap, might have potential as sustainable solutions.

How to end the poverty cycle and overcome learned helplessness is undoubtedly a complex and controversial issue, but a problem that is in desperate need of a solution. The viewpoints in *Current Controversies: Learned Helplessness, Welfare, and the Poverty Cycle* investigate the plethora of opinions and suggestions of ways to fix this age-old and pervasive problem, whether it is cutting welfare programs in favor of private charities or empowering underserved children through education. Regardless of which side of the debate the solution falls on, the ultimate answer to end poverty will require continued support and attention. As theoretical physicist Albert Einstein once said, "The world is a dangerous place, not because of those who do evil, but because of those who look on and do nothing." [7]

Notes

1. Dr. Martin Luther King, *Where Do We Go From Here: Chaos or Community?* (pp. 171-173).

2. US Census Bureau 2016 Report, "Income and Poverty in the United States: 2016." September 12, 2017. https://www.census.gov/library/publications/2017/demo/p60-259.html

3. Social Security Act of 1935 The Social Security Act (Act of August 14, 1935) [H. R. 7260] Preamble. Retrieved on May 9, 2018. https://www.ssa.gov/history/35actpre.html

4. Franklin D. Roosevelt, Annual Message to the Congress (January 4, 1935).

5. The Ross Kaminsky Show, "Speaker of the House Paul Ryan on Tax Reform and more," December 6, 2017. https://khow.iheart.com/featured/ross-kaminsky/content/2017-12-06-speaker-of-the-house-paul-ryan/

6. Bill Gates and Melinda Gates, "Our 2018 Annual Letter," February 13, 2018, https://www.gatesnotes.com/2018-Annual-Letter.

7. Robert I. Fitzhenry, *The Harper Book of Quotations*, New York, NY: Harper Collins, 1993.

CHAPTER 1

Should the Government End Welfare Entitlements?

US Poverty and Inequality Overview and Trends

John Wihbey

John Wihbey is an assistant professor of journalism and new media at Northeastern University.

Despite the fact that U.S. income inequality and poverty are playing a bigger role in political discourse, many subtle aspects of collective economic "health" continue to be under-appreciated. The Great Recession had a substantial impact on many individuals and families, and the effects are still being felt. But there are many positive counter-trends now at work, as the United States sees a comeback in many regional housing markets, the unemployment rate falls and certain aspects of the economy improve. In characterizing the state of the U.S. "economy," it is difficult to reconcile conflicting short-term, medium- and long-range trends, and for media to balance them in an accurate way.

A paper from Stanford University, "State of the Union: The Poverty and Inequality Report 2014," synthesizes economic data and academic research to paint a full picture — a "unified analysis" — of key indicators of the nation's economic health that may not receive the same visibility as GDP, aggregate growth patterns or stock market trends. Produced by the Stanford Center on Poverty and Inequality, which receives some federal funding, the report enlisted subject-area academic experts on issues such as the labor market, health, education and income trends. Overall, the data suggest a "broadly deteriorating poverty and inequality landscape."

The report's findings include:

- The economy is not delivering enough jobs, and the labor market appears to be failing by the best available measure. The way to quantify this is to look at the "prime-age employment ratio," which is the ratio of employed 25-54 year-olds to the population of that age. In tough economic times, the official unemployment rate often hides the fact that many people have stopped looking for work. By that measure, the U.S. economy is having severe trouble: "November 2013, six years after the start of the Great Recession, the proportion of all 25-54 year olds who hold jobs (i.e., 'prime age employment') was almost 5% lower than it was in December 2007, both for men and women alike."

- Poverty remains a significant problem: "The official poverty rate increased from 12.5% in 2007 to 15.0% in 2012, and the child poverty rate increased from 18.0% in 2007 to 21.8% in 2012."

- At the same time, official poverty rates don't capture the effect of government support such as food stamps (now called SNAP, or Supplemental Nutrition Assistance Program) or the Earned Income Tax Credit; if those are accounted for, the current rate would fall from 15% to 11%. A 2014 working paper done for the National Bureau of Economic Research suggests that, contrary to claims that social welfare programs have failed, social safety net programs reduced poverty by 14.5 percentage points between 1967 and 2012.

- The overall poverty rate has essentially stagnated since the 1970s, a function of two cross-cutting trends, "an economy that has increasingly left more of the poor behind and a safety net that has successfully kept more of them afloat. The primary reason that poverty remains high is that the benefits of economic growth are no longer shared by almost all workers, as they were in the quarter century after the end of World War II. In recent decades, it has been difficult for many workers, especially those with no more than a high school degree … to earn enough to keep their families out of poverty."

- The role of the recession is "more complicated than is often appreciated, with different measures of inequality yielding different conclusions about the effects of the Great Recession." This is because the social safety net and policy responses to the Great Recession performed reasonably effectively, while the capital income sources of the affluent "decline sharply." Indeed, "although the Great Recession brought about an increase in inequality for standard household income measures, it led to a flattening in consumption inequality as well as a decline in the income share going to top-income households."

- However, "there is no disagreement about what is happening in the recovery period. Since mid-2009, all measures show that inequality is rising. For example, the share of income of the top 1% had rebounded by 2012, indeed it nearly returned to the high levels from before the Great Recession. The latest, but still early, evidence on the recovery from the Great Recession also points to a very slow rebound of median incomes."

- There has been some progress in educational inequality, even as challenges remain: "The record on black-white educational inequality is mixed, with black-white disparities in academic achievement declining by approximately 40% over the last four decades, while disparities in college completion have increased over the same period." In essence, racial minorities are doing better at the K-12 levels but are struggling to achieve better results in higher education.

The report also looks at issues such as health inequality and trends in overall wealth inequality. The authors note that the "distinctively American approach is to blame our post-market institutions for the current state of affairs. The safety net is blamed for failing to make a dent in poverty; our schools are blamed for failing to eliminate income or racial disparities; and our healthcare institutions are blamed for poor health among the poor. We accordingly propose all manner of narrow-gauge safety net reforms, narrow-gauge school reforms and narrow-gauge health care reforms; and we imagine that, if only we could find the right such reforms, all would be well." However, the "very same critical scrutiny might also be applied to our economic and labor market institutions," which are failing increasingly broad swaths of the American public.

Welfare Programs Do More Harm than Good

Arthur C. Brooks

Arthur C. Brooks is president of the American Enterprise Institute (AEI). He is a contributing opinion writer for the New York Times *and the bestselling author of eleven books on topics including the role of government, fairness, economic opportunity, happiness, and the morality of free enterprise.*

In Sunday's *New York Times*, columnist Nick Kristof has an important piece that I recommend, discussing how America's social safety net has become in too many instances a net that entraps people rather than catches them when they fall:

> "This is painful for a liberal to admit, but conservatives have a point when they suggest that America's safety net can sometimes entangle people in a soul-crushing dependency. Our poverty programs do rescue many people, but other times they backfire.
>
> Some young people here don't join the military (a traditional escape route for poor, rural Americans) because it's easier to rely on food stamps and disability payments.
>
> Antipoverty programs also discourage marriage: In a means-tested program like Supplemental Security Income (SSI), a woman raising a child may receive a bigger check if she refrains from marrying that hard-working guy she likes. Yet marriage is one of the best forces to blunt poverty. In married couple households, only one child in 10 grows up in poverty, while almost half do in single-mother households.
>
> Most wrenching of all are the parents who think it's best if a child stays illiterate, because then the family may be able to claim a disability check each month.
>
> 'One of the ways you get on this program is having problems in school,' notes Richard V. Burkhauser, a Cornell University economist who co-wrote a book last year about these disability

programs. "If you do better in school, you threaten the income of the parents. It's a terrible incentive.' "

Burkhauser is an adjunct scholar at AEI, and his 2011 AEI Press book "The Declining Work and Welfare of People with Disabilities" with Mary C. Daly is a must-read for anyone interested in the convoluted world of disability policy.

I grew up in a lower middle class family, and some of our neighbors were poor–including some who were on food stamps and other forms of government assistance. We were lucky to avoid that ("lucky" in that my dad supplemented his relatively small salary by driving a bus in the summer and various other jobs). It's not that my dad was a political conservative–he wasn't–but he saw how welfare payments changed the dynamics of the families around us. Instead of helping them, it ended up hurting them.

In 1996, thanks to the increasing bipartisan understanding that welfare can hurt families (in no small part due to Charles Murray's seminal work "Losing Ground"), America reformed welfare in a way that recognized that what people need to be happy is not material handouts, but the opportunity to earn their own success.

As my colleague Nick Eberstadt shows, the growth of the entitlement state has had a deleterious impact on our national character–and fixing disability policy is an important first step in solving the larger problem.

Bravo to Nick Kristof for drawing attention to the problems that our well-intentioned social welfare and entitlement policies have caused. This shouldn't be a partisan or ideological struggle.

Education, Not Entitlements, Is the Best Way Out of Poverty

Caroline Polk

Caroline Polk is a freelance writer and editor based in Washington, DC.

Michigan welfare recipients are discouraged by the state from pursuing postsecondary degrees, according to a new report which says that state welfare policies contradict research that "overwhelmingly demonstrates that postsecondary education is the most effective way for a low-income person to become self-sufficient through long-term employment."

Forty-five percent of the welfare recipients surveyed said that education is not a priority for the welfare agency, and only 7 percent said that their caseworkers encouraged them to pursue educational goals, according to a recent report from the Center for the Education of Women at the University of Michigan.

One respondent said, "I feel like I am being penalized for going to school. No matter how I try to better my situation, all they care about is the number of hours I work." Another commented, "There is no help or reward for those of us who are trying to get a college education so we can get better jobs and get off and stay off welfare."

In addition, the report said that 13 percent of the survey respondents said that they felt pushed into low-wage jobs with little opportunity for advancement, even though they knew that they could obtain better jobs if they were able to pursue their educational goals.

Women make up 80 to 90 percent of the adults receiving federal welfare assistance nationally, and most heads of welfare households are single mothers. Before the Personal Responsibility and Work Opportunities Reconciliation Act of 1996–popularly known as

"Report Says Welfare Laws Hinder Self-Sufficiency," by Caroline Polk, Women's eNews, March 1, 2002. Reprinted by permission.

"welfare reform"–welfare recipients could receive benefits while pursuing postsecondary education. Now federal law requires states to place increasingly larger proportion of the adults receiving assistance in "approved" work activities. In addition, one-year time limits for job training and education mean that states must strictly limit the amount of time welfare recipients can spend in postsecondary education or must use their own funds to ensure access to education for recipients. To continue to receive federal assistance, single parents are required to work for at least 30 hours per week and President Bush has proposed raising the requirement to 40 hours.

Despite recent policy changes in Michigan that were intended to improve the ability of parents to pursue educational goals, data indicate that less than 2 percent of welfare recipients are enrolled in approved postsecondary education programs, according to the report, which was issued last month by the Center for the Education of Women at the University of Michigan. The survey of 98 students on welfare who were attending a variety of community colleges and four-year colleges and universities in Michigan pointed to several possible reasons for Michigan welfare recipients' low rate of participation in education and training:

- Welfare caseworkers rarely encourage welfare recipients to pursue higher education. Most recipients surveyed–89 percent–said that their caseworker provided no information about how to count education hours toward work requirements.
- It is extremely difficult for welfare recipients to juggle academics, parenting demands and work requirements. Nearly one-third of the welfare recipients surveyed reported that they had to drop out of college because they could not satisfy work requirements while enrolled in school. In Michigan, only 10 hours each of class time and study time per week can count toward work requirements and only for approved education in the last year of a two- or four-year program.

- Welfare recipients have little access to affordable, high-quality childcare. State policy provides childcare assistance only in limited situations and only in connection with educational programs that has been approved by local welfare agencies. Moreover, childcare is available only during class time, not for the hours parents need to study.
- Welfare recipients receive inaccurate and inconsistent information about educational options, when they receive any information at all. Moreover, the focus is on high school or passing an high school degree equivalency exam, not postsecondary education.

Beth Sullivan, a program manager for policy and advocacy at the Center for the Education of Women, said that Michigan Gov. John Engler's policy has been to get people into jobs as soon as possible and education is viewed as a delay to getting people into work.

"There hasn't been the appreciation that education can increase job possibilities," she said.

Douglas Besharov, a professor at the University of Maryland School of Public Affairs and a welfare researcher at the American Enterprise Institute for Public Policy Research, sees the decline in welfare recipients enrolled in postsecondary education as a natural by-product of welfare reform's success in decreasing the welfare rolls.

"A lot of women who leave welfare don't leave for work; they leave for marriage, education, or other reasons," he said. Moreover, Besharov said, the studies showing a correlation between college education and wages suffer from selection bias. "Women who go to college tend to have more going for them in the first place. Think how much it takes to graduate from college."

Other Studies Find Single Parents Funneled into Low-Wage Jobs

The Michigan study is the latest in a series of reports assessing whether the 1996 welfare law assisted single parents in finding long-term financial self-sufficiency. Last year, the Institute for Women's Policy Research found that women tend to be pushed toward low-wage jobs in customer service, patient care, clerical, child care, and restaurants. It also found that training programs emphasize traditional "women's work" in cosmetology, hospitality, and childcare, rather than nontraditional fields, such as the building trades or the pursuit of education beyond high school.

"Access to postsecondary education is very limited across the board," said M. K. Tally of the Institute for Women's Policy Research. "The focus on 'work first' has diminished the number of people pursuing education."

Liz Accles, national coordinator of the Welfare Made A Difference National Campaign, which promotes a more supportive welfare system and educates the public about the consequences of punitive welfare policies, noted that welfare reform has had similar effects in New York as in Michigan.

Hunter College's Welfare Rights Initiative, a program based in a college that is part of the City University of New York, reports that 28,000 students in the City University of New York system were receiving welfare in 1995, but now less than 10,000 are still enrolled in CUNY programs. "These were people motivated, interested, able to be in school. Their chance of getting a job that could sustain their families was undermined," Accles said.

"The debate is twisted," Accles said, noting that at the same time that Congress authorized restrictions on the ability of welfare recipients to obtain higher education, it also approved tax-free educational savings accounts and tax deductions for student loans that made it easier for others to attend colleges and universities. "There is a policy disconnect and it's because of a stereotyping of people on welfare as being different from everyone else."

Sullivan at the Center for the Education of Women added that since "students receiving public assistance pull their own weight by being employed at work-study jobs and taking out loans, just like other college students," ultimately Michigan and other states would save money by facilitating postsecondary education for welfare recipients.

For every parent receiving child-care assistance who completes higher education, Michigan saves an average of $6,696 per year in childcare benefits alone that it would otherwise spend to help that parent if he or she remained in a low-wage job. In addition, the report points out, states benefit from increased tax revenues from workers making good wages.

Private Charity Is More Flexible and Generous than Government Welfare

Michael Tanner and Tad DeHaven

Michael Tanner is a Cato Institute senior fellow. He heads research on a variety of domestic policies with a particular emphasis on poverty and social welfare policy, health care reform, and social security. Tad DeHaven was a budget analyst on federal and state budget issues for the Cato Institute.

The federal government funds a large range of subsidy programs for low-income Americans, from food stamps to Medicaid. This essay examines Temporary Assistance for Needy Families (TANF), which is a joint federal-state cash assistance program for low-income families with children. When most people think of "welfare," they are thinking of this program.

Since a major welfare reform in 1996, federal spending on TANF has been held fairly constant at somewhat less than $20 billion per year.[1] The 2009 American Recovery and Reinvestment Act provided an additional $5 billion in federal funding over several years. About 1.8 million families receive TANF payments each month.[2]

Before 1996, federal welfare was an open-ended entitlement that encouraged long-term dependency, and there was widespread agreement that it was a terrible failure. It neither reduced poverty nor helped the poor become self-sufficient. It encouraged out-of-wedlock births and weakened the work ethic. The pathologies it engendered were passed from generation to generation.

The welfare reforms of 1996 were dramatic, but the federal government still runs an array of welfare programs that are expensive and damaging. The federal government should phase-out its role in TANF and related welfare programs and leave low-income assistance programs to state governments, or better yet, the private sector.

Government welfare cannot provide the same flexibility and diversity as private charities. Private aid organizations have a better understanding that true charity starts with individuals making better life choices. Federal involvement in welfare has generated an expensive mess of paperwork and bureaucracy while doing little to solve the problem of long-term poverty.

[…]

Breaking up Families

The tragedy of government welfare programs is not just wasted taxpayer money but wasted lives. The effects of welfare in encouraging the break-up of low-income families have been extensively documented. The primary way that those with low incomes can advance in the market economy is to get married, stay married, and work—but welfare programs have created incentives to do the opposite.

The number of single-parent families has risen dramatically since the 1960s. The most important reason for the rise in single-parent families is births to unmarried women. In 1965, less than 8 percent of all births were out of wedlock. Today the figure is 39 percent.[3]

The policy concern about the increase in out-of-wedlock births is not a question of private morality. The concern is that out-of-wedlock childbearing remains overwhelmingly concentrated at the lowest rungs of the socio-economic ladder. Having a child out of wedlock at an early age for someone without career skills can mean a lifetime of poverty.

Of more than 20 major studies of the issue, more than three-quarters show a significant link between welfare benefit levels and out-of-wedlock childbearing.[4] Higher benefit levels mean higher out-of-wedlock births. Children living with single mothers are seven times more likely to be poor than those living with two parents.[5]

Welfare removes some of the negative economic consequences of out-of-wedlock births, and thus encourages more such births. More than 20 percent of single-mothers start on welfare because they have an out-of-wedlock birth,[6] and 75 percent of government aid to children through means-tested programs like TANF goes to single-parent families.[7] Moreover, once on welfare, single mothers find it difficult to get off, and they tend to stay on welfare for longer periods than other recipients.[8]

Focusing solely on the out-of-wedlock birthrate may actually understate the problem. In the past, women who gave birth out of wedlock frequently married the fathers of their children after the birth. As many as 85 percent of unwed mothers, in the 1950s, ultimately married the fathers of their children.[9] Therefore, while technically born out of wedlock, the children were still likely to grow up in intact two-parent families.

However, the increasing availability and value of welfare have made such marriages less attractive for unwed mothers. If the father is unskilled and has poor employment prospects, a welfare check may seem a preferable alternative. Studies indicate that young mothers and pregnant women are less likely to marry the fathers of their children in states with higher welfare benefits.[10] Nonetheless, 70 percent of poor single mothers would no longer be in poverty if they married their children's father.[11]

Welfare is also likely to entrap the next generation as well. The attitudes and habits that lead to welfare dependency are transmitted the same way as other parent-to-child pathologies, such as alcoholism and child abuse. Although it is true that the majority of children raised on welfare will not receive welfare themselves, the rate of welfare dependence for children raised on it is far higher than for their non-welfare counterparts.

Children raised on welfare are likely to have lower incomes as adults than children not raised on welfare. The more welfare received by a child's family, the lower that child's earnings as an adult tend to be, even holding constant such other factors as race, family structure, and education.[12] According to one study, nearly 20 percent of daughters from families that were "highly dependent" on welfare became "highly dependent" themselves, whereas only 3 percent of daughters from non-welfare households became "highly dependent" on welfare.[13]

Disincentives to Work

The choice of welfare over work is often a rational decision based on economic incentives. Empirical studies confirm that welfare is a disincentive for work. For example, an analysis of interstate variation in labor force participation by economists Richard Vedder, Lowell Gallaway, and Robert Lawson found that such participation declined as welfare benefits increased.[14] Similarly, Robert Moffitt of Brown University found that the work effort of welfare recipients was reduced by as much as 30 percent.[15]

Such studies may understate the work disincentive of welfare because they consider only a small portion of the total package of federal and state welfare benefits. Benefits available to people in the welfare system that are not available to the working poor create an incentive to go on welfare and remain in the program once enrolled.[16] For example, one study shows that education and training programs available under TANF may induce people to go on welfare.[17]

Perhaps most troubling of all is the psychological attitude toward work that can develop among those on welfare. Studies have found that the poor on welfare do not have a strong sense that they need to take charge of their own lives or find work to become self-sufficient.[18] Indeed, they often have a feeling that the government has an obligation to provide for them.

Of course, these psychological effects are also true for other government subsidy recipients, including farmers, the elderly, and businesses that are hooked on federal hand-outs of one sort or another. Farmers that are major subsidy recipients, for example, are less likely to make tough decisions to cut costs or diversify their income sources because they know they will be bailed out if market conditions sour on them. It is not healthy for any group in society to depend on government welfare for their long-term survival, whether they are farmers or poor inner-city families.

Relationship to Crime Levels

Children from single-parent families are more likely to become involved in criminal activity. Research indicates a direct correlation between crime rates and the number of single-parent families in a neighborhood.[19] As welfare contributes to the rise in out-of-wedlock births, it thus also contributes to higher levels of criminal activity.

A Maryland National Association for the Advancement of Colored People (NAACP) report concluded that "the ready access to a lifetime of welfare and free social service programs is a major contributory factor to the crime problems we face today."[20] The NAACP's conclusion is confirmed by additional academic research. For example, research by M. Anne Hill and June O'Neill shows that a 50-percent increase in welfare and food stamp benefits led to a 117-percent increase in the crime rate among young black men.[21]

Barbara Whitehead noted in an article in the *Atlantic Monthly*:

> The relationship [between single-parent families and crime] is so strong that controlling for family configuration erases the relationship between race and crime and between low income and crime. This conclusion shows up time and again in the literature. The nation's mayors, as well as police officers, social workers, probation officers, and court officials, consistently point to family breakup as the most important source of rising rates of crime.[22]

Welfare leads to increased crime by contributing to the marginalization of young men in society. As author George Gilder noted, "The welfare culture tells the man he is not a necessary part of the family."[23] Marriage and family have long been considered civilizing influences on young men. Whether or not causation can be proven, it is true that unwed fathers are more likely to use drugs and become involved in criminal behavior than are other men.[24]

Replacing Welfare with Private Charity

The 1996 welfare reforms were a step in the right direction, but much more needs to be done. The next step should be to transfer full responsibility for funding and administering welfare programs to the states. The states would have freedom to innovate with their low-income programs and would have strong incentives to reduce taxpayer costs and maximize work incentives.

The ultimate reform goal, however, should be to eliminate the entire system of low-income welfare for individuals who are able to work. That means eliminating not just TANF but also food stamps, subsidized housing, and other programs. Individuals unwilling to support themselves through the job market would have to rely on the support of family, church, community, or private charity.

What would happen to the poor if welfare were eliminated? Without the negative incentives created by the welfare state, fewer people would be poor. There would also likely be fewer children born into poverty. Studies suggest that women do make rational decisions about whether to have children, and thus a reduction in welfare benefits would reduce the likelihood of their becoming pregnant or having children out of wedlock.[24]

In addition, some poor women who had children out of wedlock would put the children up for adoption. The government should encourage that by eliminating the present regulatory and bureaucratic barriers to adoption. Other unmarried women who gave birth would not be able to afford to live independently and they would have to live with their families or boyfriends. Some would choose to marry the fathers of their children.

Despite the positive social effects of ending government welfare, there will still be many people who make mistakes and find themselves in tough situations. Americans are an enormously generous people, and there is a vast amount of private charitable support available, especially for people truly in need.

Private charity is superior to government welfare for many reasons. Private charities are able to individualize their approaches to the circumstances of poor people. By contrast, government programs are usually designed in a one-size-fits-all manner that treats all recipients alike. Most government programs rely on the simple provision of cash or services without any attempt to differentiate between the needs of recipients.

The eligibility requirements for government welfare programs are arbitrary and cannot be changed to fit individual circumstances. Consequently, some people in genuine need do not receive assistance, while benefits often go to people who do not really need them. Surveys of people with low incomes generally indicate a higher level of satisfaction with private charities than with government welfare agencies.[25]

Private charities also have a better record of actually delivering aid to recipients because they do not have as much administrative overhead, inefficiency, and waste as government programs. A lot of the money spent on federal and state social welfare programs never reaches recipients because it is consumed by fraud and bureaucracy.

Audits of TANF spending by the Health and Human Services' Inspector General have found huge levels of "improper payments," meaning errors, abuse, and fraud. In 2005, the state of New York had an improper TANF payment rate of 28 percent and Michigan had an improper payment rate of 40 percent.[26] During 2006 and 2007, Ohio had an improper payment rate in TANF of 21 percent.[27] There are similar high levels of waste in other states.[28]

Another advantage of private charity is that aid is much more likely to be targeted to short-term emergency assistance, not long-term dependency. Private charity provides a safety net, not a way of life. Moreover, private charities may demand that the poor change their behavior in exchange for assistance, such as stopping drug abuse, looking for a job, or avoiding pregnancy. Private charities are more likely than government programs to offer counseling and one-on-one follow-up, rather than simply providing a check.

In sum, private charities typically require a different attitude on the part of recipients. They are required to consider the aid they receive not as an entitlement, but as a gift carrying reciprocal obligations. At the same time, private charities require that donors become directly involved in monitoring program performance.

Those who oppose replacing government welfare with private charity often argue that there will not be enough charitable giving to make up for the loss of government benefits. However, that assumes that private charity would simply recreate existing government programs. But the advantage of private and decentralized charity is that less expensive and more innovative ways of helping smaller groups of truly needy people would be developed.

If large amounts of aid continue to be needed, there is every reason to believe that charitable giving in the nation would increase in the absence of government welfare. In every area of society and the economy, we have seen that government expansion tends to "crowd out" private voluntary activities. So, in reverse, when the government shrinks, private activities would fill in the gaps.

A number of studies have demonstrated such a government crowd-out effect in low-income assistance.[29] Charitable giving declined dramatically during the 1970s, as the Great Society programs of the 1960s were expanding. The decline in giving leveled out in the 1980s as welfare spending began to level out and the public was deluged with news stories about supposed cutbacks in federal programs. Then, after the passage of welfare reform in 1996, there was a large spike in private giving.[30] Studies have also shown that when particular charities start receiving government funds, there is a decrease in private donations to those charities.[31]

Americans are the most generous people on earth, contributing more than $300 billion a year to organized private charities. In addition, they volunteer more than 8 billion hours a year to charitable activities, with an estimated value of about $158 billion.[32] Americans donate countless dollars and countless efforts toward providing informal help to families, neighbors, and others in need. There is every reason to believe that the elimination of government welfare would bring a very positive response both from recipients of government welfare and from Americans wanting to help those who are truly in need.

Notes

[1] *Budget of the United States Government: Fiscal Year 2011, Historical Tables*, Table 12.3.

[2] Department of Health and Human Services, «2009 TANF Report to Congress,» June 2009, p. X-6.

[3] Department of Health and Human Services, "Indicators of Welfare Dependence: Annual Report to Congress, 2008," p. III-36.

[4] Ron Haskins, "Does Welfare Encourage Illegitimacy? The Case Just Closed. The Answer is Yes," American Enterprise Institute, January 1996.

[5] Robert Rector, Heritage Foundation, Testimony before the Subcommittee on Human Resources of the House Committee on Ways and Means, February 10, 2005.

[6] Department of Health and Human Services, "Indicators of Welfare Dependence: Annual Report to Congress, 2008," p. II-33.

[7] Robert Rector, Heritage Foundation, Testimony before the Subcommittee on Human Resources of the House Committee on Ways and Means, February 10, 2005.

[8] Jodie Levin-Epstein, Christine Grisham, and Maya Batchelder, "Regarding Teen Pregnancy Prevention and Teen Parenting Provisions in the Temporary Assistance for Needy Families Block Grant," Center for Law and Social Policy, November 30, 2001.

[9] Marvin Olasky, *The Tragedy of American Compassion* (Washington: Regnery, 1992), p. 186.

[10] Shelley Lundberg and Robert Plotnick, "Effects of State Welfare, Abortion, and Family Planning Policies on Premarital Childbearing among White Adolescents," *Family Planning Perspectives* 22, no. 6 (1990): 246–51.

[11] Robert Rector, Heritage Foundation, Testimony before the Subcommittee on Human Resources of the House Committee on Ways and Means, February 10, 2005.

[12] Mary Corcoran et al., "The Association between Men's Economic Status and Their Family and Community Origins," *Journal of Human Resources* 27, no. 4 (Fall 1992): 575–601.

[13] Greg Duncan and Martha Hill, "Welfare Dependence Within and Across Generations," *Science*, January 29, 1988, pp. 467–71.

[14] Richard Vedder, Lowell Gallaway, and Robert Lawson, "Why People Work: An Examination of Interstate Variation in Labor Force Participation," *Journal of Labor Research* 12, no. 1 (Winter 1991): 47–59.

[15] Robert Moffitt, "Incentive Effects of the U.S. Welfare System: A Review," *Journal of Economic Literature* 30, no. 1 (March 1992): 17.

[16] David Card, Philip Robins, and Winston Lin, "Would Financial Incentives for Leaving Welfare Lead Some People to Stay on Welfare Longer?" National Bureau of Economic Research Working Paper no. 6449, March 1998.

[17] Cited in David Card, Philip Robins, and Winston Lin, "Would Financial Incentives for Leaving Welfare Lead Some People to Stay on Welfare Longer: An Experimental Evaluation of 'Entry Effects' in the Self-Sufficiency Project," National Bureau of Economic Research Working Paper no. 6449, March 1998.

[18] For example, see Ken Auletta, *The Underclass* (New York: Random House, 1982).

[19] Douglas Smith and G. Roger Jarjoura, "Social Structure and Criminal Victimization," *Journal of Research in Crime and Delinquency* 25, no. 1 (February 1988): 27–52.

[20] John L. Wright, Marge Green, and Leroy Warren Jr., "An Assessment of Crime in Maryland Today," Maryland State Conference of Branches, NAACP, Annapolis, February 1994, p. 7.

[21] M. Anne Hill and June O'Neill, "Underclass Behaviors in the United States: Measurement and Analysis of Determinants," Baruch College, City University of New York, August 1993, p. 73.

[22] Barbara Defoe Whitehead, «Dan Quayle Was Right,» *Atlantic Monthly*, April 1993, p. 50.

[23] Cited in Tom Bethell, "They Had a Dream: The Politics of Welfare Reform," *National Review,* August 23, 1993, p. 33.

[24] Robert Lerman, "Unwed Fathers: Who Are They?" *American Enterprise,* September-October 1993, pp. 32–37.

[25] Robert Wuthnow, Conrad Hackett, and Becky Yang Hsu, "The Effectiveness and Trustworthiness of Faith-Based and Other Service Organizations: A Study of Recipients' Perceptions" (paper presented at a conference on "The Role of Faith-Based Organizations in the Social Welfare System," Washington, DC, March 6–7, 2003).

[26] See Department of Health and Human Services, Office of Inspector General, "Review of Improper Temporary Assistance for Needy Families Basic Assistance Payments in New York State for July 1 through December 31, 2005," October 31, 2007; and Department of Health and Human Services, Office of Inspector General, "Review of Improper Temporary Assistance for Needy Families Basic Assistance Payments in Michigan for July 1 through December 31, 2005," November 13, 2007.

[27] See Department of Health and Human Services, Office of Inspector General, "Review of Improper Temporary Assistance for Needy Families Basic Assistance Payments in Ohio for April 1, 2006 through March 31, 2007," July 15, 2008.

[28] See Department of Health and Human Services, Office of Inspector General, «Review of Improper Temporary Assistance for Needy Families Basic Assistance Payments in California for April 1, 2006 through March 31, 2007,» September 2008.

[29] See, for example, Russell Roberts, «A Positive Model of Private Charity and Public Transfers,» *Journal of Political Economy* 92 (1984): 136–48; and B. A. Abrams and M. D. Schmitz, «The Crowding out Effect of Government Transfers on Private Charitable Contributions,» *Public Choice,* no. 1 (1978): 28–40.

[30] American Association of Fundraising Counsel (AAFRC) Trust for Philanthropy, «Giving USA 2002,» Indianapolis, IN, June 20, 2002.

[31] Christopher Horne, David Van Slyke, and Janet Johnson, "Attitudes for Public Funding for Faith-Based Organizations and the Potential Impact on Private Giving" (paper presented to a conference on "The Role of Faith-Based Organizations in the Social Welfare System," Washington, DC, March 7–8, 2003).

[32] Ret Boney, «U.S. Giving Hits Record $306 Billion,» *Philanthropy Journal* online, June 23, 2008. And see Corporation for National and Community Service, "Volunteering in America," July 2008, p. 2.

The Proof Is in the Pudding: Welfare Programs Reduce Poverty

Jana Kasperkevic

Jana Kasperkevic is a digital reporter for Marketplace, *where she is based in the New York City bureau.*

F ood stamps. Unemployment benefits. Social security. Earned income tax credits.

Do these social welfare programs work? Yes, according to a new study from the Pew Charitable Trusts.

Safety nets like food stamps prevent millions more people from struggling to put food on the table, says Jake Grovum, who analyzed the data for the Pew Charitable Trusts.

Consider Grovum's findings:

- For people of all ages, the official poverty rate in the US was 14.5%. That's equivalent to 45.3 million people.
- Without food stamps, the poverty rate would be 17.10% – another 8 million Americans would be living in poverty.
- Without social security, the poverty rate for Americans 65 and older would be 52.67% instead of the current 14.6%.
- Without tax credits like the federal earned income tax credit, poverty for children under 18 would be 22.8% instead of the official poverty rate of 19.9%.

These numbers are important. US lawmakers have long struggled to show exactly how and where certain types of government assistance are helping Americans stay out of poverty.

Nobody, on the right or the left, wants more people to live in poverty. Yet America has a dismal record on poverty for an advanced nation. Already, over 14% of US households have experienced food insecurity. One in seven Americans live in poverty, including one in five US children. Of all the millions of unemployed people in the country, fully one-third have been out of work for 27 weeks or more.

Where the opinions divide is how to address the problem. Republicans including Paul Ryan have advocated cutting and consolidating government programs. Congress put that belief into legislation last year, cutting both food stamps and unemployment benefits.

The assumption in the slash-and-burn approach is that poor Americans have no one to blame but themselves for their poverty, and they only need more discipline to get out of their circumstances. Welfare skeptics find the accounts of those struggling "another sob story" and wonder why more people can't just bootstrap themselves.

If only the poor could be more organized. As Ryan put it in his poverty plan,

> Providers must be held accountable, and so should recipients. Each beneficiary will sign a contract with consequences for failing to meet the agreed-upon benchmarks. At the same time, there should also be incentives for people to go to work. Under each life plan, if the individual meets the benchmarks ahead of schedule, then he or she could be rewarded.

Meanwhile Democrats and advocates for the poor cite the fact that downward mobility has become a big factor in the current manifestation of American poverty.

"For most of the American public, this downturn in the last six, seven years was a wake-up call because people in their families that they knew lost their home, were out of work for a longer period of time and they looked at that and went: 'Holy cow, maybe we do need government assistance when something like that happens,'" Dave Reaney, executive director of the Bay Area Food Bank in Alabama, told the *Guardian*. "I think that's why a majority of Americans today do feel that safety nets are important."

What has complicated the discussion for years is that the official poverty rate, based on the income of American households, does not tell the true story of America's poor.

"A lot of people don't remember that [the official poverty rate] doesn't include things like food stamps and other programs that are really important and actually do help a lot of people," Grovum says.

That is why, in 2010, the US government decided to introduce yet another measure of poverty: the supplemental poverty rate, which takes into consideration consumer spending on necessities like food, shelter and utilities as well as any assistance that they might receive.

Since the supplemental poverty measure also considers cost of living in different places around the country like housing and medical expenses, it more accurately captures the way people experience poverty.

"The one thing that can get missed when you are talking about poverty rates is the way that different factors around the country can play into that," explains Grovum. "You have states where it's expensive to live and it's really different to be poor there than it is in states where it's less expensive to live."

He adds:

In some sense, it's kind of missing this whole system that we have set up for people who are poor. The other measure helps put that in context and helps people remember that there are these programs that help people and how they help them.

Take California. If one were to account for all the expenses accrued and benefits received by the 38 million people living in the Golden State, the real poverty rate would be closer to 23.4% than 16%, which is the official poverty rate. In New Mexico, on the other hand, the supplemental poverty rate, 16%, is much lower than the official poverty rate, 21.5%. According to Grovum, the poverty rate was lower under the supplemental measure than it was under the official measure in 26 states.

Unfortunately, the official poverty thresholds will still be used to award government assistance. The new measure, in the meantime, will be used to measure the health of the US economy and to better understand the effects of government assistance, according to the US census bureau website.

The upshot: especially in post-recession America, these so-called "hand-outs" are exactly what keeps millions of Americans from living in deeper poverty.

Battling the Common Myths
of Poverty and Behavior

Christopher Jencks and Kathryn Edin

Christopher Jencks is the Malcolm Wiener Professor of Social Policy at Harvard University's Kennedy School of Government. Kathryn Edin is an assistant professor of sociology at the University of Pennsylvania.

Affluent adults seldom consider the possibility that others may have to choose between accepting public assistance or dying childless. We prefer to believe that if everyone would act responsibly, they would all be able to support their children without government help. We are particularly keen on three forms of responsible behavior: delaying parenthood until you are in your twenties, getting married before you have children, and staying in school.

But even if everyone pursued these goals single-mindedly, a significant minority of the population still could not afford children without some kind of government help.

[...]

Fairy Tale #1: If Teen Mothers Simply Held Off Parenthood Until Their Twenties, They Would Have Enough Money to Raise a Family

TV commentators, magazine articles, and public service advertisements have claimed for years that teenage motherhood ("children having children") is a major cause of poverty. The administration apparently endorses this view, claiming that "welfare dependency could be significantly reduced if more young people delayed childbearing until both parents were ready to assume the responsibility of raising children." The fact sheet accompanying the administration's welfare proposals supports this claim with a dramatic statistic: 40 percent of

"Do Poor Women Have a Right to Bear Children?" by Christopher Jencks and Kathryn Edin, The American Prospect, 1995. Reprinted by permission.

current welfare recipients had their first child before their nineteenth birthday.

The administration is right when it claims that early childbearing is correlated with subsequent welfare receipt. But everyone knows, or ought to know, that a correlation of this kind is not sufficient to prove causation. Women who have babies as teenagers differ from those who wait in a multitude of other ways, many of which affect their economic prospects. To begin with, teen mothers tend to come from troubled homes. In an effort to separate the effects of family background from the age at which women became mothers, Arlene Geronimus from the University of Michigan and Sanders Korenman from the University of Minnesota compared sisters raised in the same family. They found that women who had had their first child while they were teenagers ended up only a little poorer than their sisters who had waited.

Family background aside, most teen mothers have also had trouble in school. Their grades and test scores have usually been below average, and they are more likely to have been in disciplinary trouble than women who delay motherhood. Many attend schools where below-average students are written off at an early age. Because of these problems, many teenage mothers quit school even before they become pregnant. When a teenager comes from a troubled family, has learned little in school, and has left school without graduating, she is unlikely to be economically self-sufficient no matter how long she delays motherhood.

Fairy Tale #2: If Single Mothers Got Married, They Wouldn't Need Welfare

Those who see welfare dependency as a byproduct of irresponsibility argue that even dropouts with low test scores could stay off welfare if only they would marry before having children. Once again the correlation is clear. Women who have a child out of wedlock are at least three times as likely to need welfare as women who have their children while married. But that does not mean two-thirds of unwed welfare recipients could have made themselves self-sufficient by marrying the man who fathered their children.

If a would-be mother wants to stay off welfare, she has to find a husband who can pull his weight economically. Although the federal poverty threshold for a married couple with two children is currently about $15,000, a two-parent family in which both adults work and pay for child care needs at least $20,000 a year (and probably closer to $25,000) to cover its basic needs. (This estimate is based on studies of family budgets in four big cities, which we discuss in more detail later.) If family income falls below that level, the mother is usually better off on welfare, where she gets both Medicaid and food stamps and has no husband to support, no child care bills, and no work-related expenses. In families where both parents work, the man usually earns about 60 percent of the income. Thus, for marriage to make a mother better off than she would be on welfare, her husband must usually earn at least $12,000 a year. There are not enough men (or jobs) like that to go around.

In 1989, just before the recent recession, there were 22 million American women between the ages of 25 and 34. About 20 million of these women either had a child or wanted one. Fewer than 16 million men of the same age had annual incomes above $12,000. Some of these men were gay or reluctant to marry for other reasons. Others were philanderers, wife beaters, substance abusers, or child molesters. By traditional American standards the number of acceptable husbands was probably no more than two-thirds the number of women who wanted children.

Marrying a man with an unstable work history or low wages is not a good formula for avoiding welfare. These days more than half the women who marry such a man can expect their marriage to end in divorce; and when that happens their ex-husbands are unlikely to be either willing or able to pay much child support.

Fairy Tale #3: If Teen Mothers Finished High School Before Having Kids, They Could Get Good Jobs

Recognizing that marriage is no guarantee of economic self-sufficiency, American women have been staying in school longer and acquiring more specialized occupational skills than they did a generation ago. Nonetheless, only a minority can support children on their earnings alone. In 1989, a single working mother with two children needed about $15,000 worth of goods and services to make ends meet. Less than half the 25- to 34-year-old women who worked in 1989 earned that much.

The nature of this problem becomes clearer if we look at the National Longitudinal Survey of Youth, which began following a representative sample of 14- to 21-year-olds in 1979. At the beginning of the study, participants were given the Armed Forces Qualification Test (AFQT), which measures vocabulary, reading comprehension, computational skills, and ability to reason quantitatively. When Gary Burtless looked at 25-year-old women who were getting AFDC, he found that 72 percent of them had scored in the bottom quarter of their age group on the AFQT. Half were also high school dropouts.

While high school dropouts with low test scores often found some kind of work, their wages averaged only $5.50 to $6.00 an hour (in 1991 dollars). Nor did their earnings rise as they accumulated more labor market experience. After adjusting for inflation, Burtless found that these women earned only 25 cents an hour more when they were 29 years old than when they were 21. Nor does earning a high school equivalency certificate (technically known as a Certificate of General Educational Development, or simply a "GED") seem to increase their earnings. Recent research shows that high school dropouts with a GED earn no more than those who lack one. Nor does the short-term job training that most states now offer welfare recipients boost their hourly wages— though it does help them find work, so the money is not wasted.

Women with low test scores who finish high school on schedule do earn $1 to $1.25 an hour more than those who drop out. But that does not mean today's dropouts would earn an extra $1.25 if they stayed in school. Much would depend on what they did with their time while they were in school. Adolescents are desperate for respect. Those who are not good at schoolwork usually find that the easiest way to maintain their self-respect, at least in the short run, is not to work hard but to define school as "irrelevant" and find friends who do the same. If a teenage girl does no schoolwork, it is hard to see how keeping her enrolled will make her more valuable to her future employers. Having a diploma may help her get a job that someone else would otherwise get, but if everyone stays in school this "sheepskin effect" will disappear. Keeping everyone in school for 12 years will only boost wages if it makes the former dropouts more productive, and productivity is unlikely to rise unless students are learning something.

[...]

Welfare Reform Celebrates Many Successes

Kay S. Hymowitz

Kay S. Hymowitz is the William E. Simon Fellow at the Manhattan Institute and a contributing editor for City Journal. *She writes extensively on childhood, family issues, poverty, and cultural change in America.*

Welfare reform celebrates its tenth anniversary this year, and celebrates seems the right word. As most readers know, Temporary Assistance for Needy Families (TANF) ended the much-despised Depression-era federal entitlement to cash benefits for needy single mothers, replacing it with short-term, work-oriented programs designed and run by individual states. Its success has surprised just about everyone, supporters and naysayers alike.

So it seems a good time to remember the drama—make that melodrama—that the bill unleashed in 1996. Cries from Democrats of "anti-family," "anti-child," "mean-spirited," echoed through the Capitol, as did warnings of impending Third World–style poverty: "children begging for money, children begging for food, eight- and nine-year-old prostitutes," as New Jersey senator Frank Lautenberg put it. "They are coming for the children," Congressman John Lewis of Georgia wailed—"coming for the poor, coming for the sick, the elderly and disabled." Congressman William Clay of Missouri demanded, "What's next? Castration?" Senator Ted Kennedy called it "legislative child abuse," Senator Chris Dodd, "unconscionable," Senator Daniel Patrick Moynihan—in what may well be the lowest point of an otherwise miraculous career—"something approaching an Apocalypse."

Other Washington bigwigs took up the cry. Marion Wright Edelman of the Children's Defense Fund called the bill "national child abandonment" and likened it to the burning of Vietnamese

"How Welfare Reform Worked," by Kay S. Hymowitz, Manhattan Institute for Policy Research, 2006. The piece first appeared in City Journal. Reprinted by permission.

villages. Immediately after President Clinton signed the bill, some of his top appointees quit in protest, including Edelman's husband, Peter, who let loose with an article in *The Atlantic Monthly* titled, "The Worst Thing Bill Clinton Has Done." No less appalled, the *Chicago Tribune* seconded Congresswoman Carol Moseley Braun's branding the bill an "abomination." And while in 2004 the New York Times lauded the legislation as "one of the acclaimed successes of the past decade," the editors seem to have forgotten that they were irately against it before they were for it, pronouncing it "draconian" and a "sad day for poor children."

It's worth recalling the outcry at this anniversary moment, not in order to have a gotcha-fest, pleasurable as such an exercise can be. The truth is that many of welfare reform's promoters were not spot-on in their predictions, either, and their expectations require some Monday-morning quarterbacking, too. But the apocalyptic scaremongering of reform opponents on the one hand, and the relative benignity of the bill's consequences on the other, prompt the obvious question: How is it that so many intelligent, well-intentioned people, including many experts who made up the late twentieth century's Best and Brightest, were so mistaken—mistaken not just in the way a weatherman who overestimates the strength of a snowstorm is mistaken, but fundamentally, intrinsically, and epistemologically *wrong*?

Before examining *why* so many people were wrong, let's look at exactly *how* they were wrong—an easy task, given the Everest of data on welfare reform's aftermath. TANF did not include a federal jobs program for the poor—though many wanted it to—but it has ended up being a WPA for social scientists, who have been busily crunching just about every number that happened to wander anywhere near a welfare recipient for the past ten years.

The most striking outcome has been the staggering decline in the welfare rolls, so large it has left even reform enthusiasts agog. At their peak in 1994—the rolls began to shrink before 1996, because many states had already instituted experimental reform programs—there were 5.1 million families on Aid to Families with Dependent Children, the old program. Almost immediately, the numbers went into freefall, and by 2004 they were down by 60 percent, to fewer than 2 million. A lot of reform opponents—the unreformed, so to speak—tried to chalk this up to the booming economy of the later 1990s. But according to former congressional staffer Ron Haskins, author of a history of the reform due out this fall, that doesn't make sense: in the 41 years between 1953 and 1994, he points out, the welfare rolls had declined only five times, and only once (between 1977 and 1979) for two years in a row. Compare that with the present case, when the rolls continued their fall even after a recession began in 2001, and when 2004 marked the tenth continuous year of decline.

Caseload declines are all well and good, but what caused opponents—and many proponents as well—to lose sleep was what would happen to women and their children once they left the dole. There were four chief concerns: First, would welfare leavers find jobs? Second, would they sink even deeper into poverty? Third, would their children be harmed? And fourth, would the states take advantage of the wide flexibility the bill gave them on implementation to join what many anticipated would be a "race to the bottom"?

So let's consider concern number one: Did women who left the rolls actually go to work? The answer is: more than almost anyone had predicted. According to one Urban Institute study, 63 percent of leavers were working in the peak year of 1999. True, some studies showed numbers only in the high fifties, but even these findings were much better than expected.

Nevertheless, a lot of skeptics still weren't biting. It was the luck of a boom economy, they said; just wait until the job market sours. Well, the recession came in 2001, and though it was no picnic, it was—once again—nothing like what had been feared. As of 2002, 57 percent of leavers continued to punch a time clock. That, the critics warned, was only because the first recipients to leave welfare were likely to be the most competent. Just wait until we're dealing with the most dysfunctional, those who have the most "barriers to employment"—from limited education or work experience to English-language deficiency or mental disability.

But even there the news was encouraging. The Urban Institute kept a close eye on the caseload composition in welfare reform's early years and found that the proportion of highly disadvantaged women was no greater in 1999 than in 1997. A 2003 study by June O'Neill and Anne Hill found a large increase in the employment of some of these women: for example, in 1992 only 31 percent of young single mothers who were high school dropouts were employed; by 2000, 50 percent had jobs. And none of this takes into account the women who under the previous regime might have gone on welfare but, after TANF, with its time limits and hassles, never did. The percentage of employed single mothers rose, in the years following reform, from 45 percent in 1990 to 62 percent in 2005—nearing the employment rate of their married counterparts.

What about concern number two—that welfare mothers would sink deeper into poverty? Shortly before TANF passed, the Urban Institute released a report, solicited by a wavering Clinton administration, warning that welfare reform could impoverish an additional 2 million people. Reform Jeremiahs waved the report around as scientific proof of their worst fears. Even if some welfare mothers did find jobs, they argued, they would merely be stocking shelves at Duane Reade or making hotel beds, the proverbial "dead-end jobs" that would leave them worse off than on the dole.

Though a lot of women did take low-paying service jobs, the unreformed got this one wrong, too. For one thing, they failed to consider the Earned Income Tax Credit, whose expansion in 1993 meant a 40 percent boost in annual earnings for a minimum-wage worker with two kids. Most leavers, though, were doing better than minimum wage. In 2002, the same Urban Institute that had predicted TANF disaster found that the median hourly wage for working former recipients was around $8 an hour. Moreover, O'Neill and Hill discovered that, just as with most other people, the longer recipients were in the job market, the more they earned; four years off welfare, only 4 percent of working single mothers—and only 8 percent of high school dropouts who were single mothers—were earning minimum wage or less.

As a result, most welfare leavers had more money than when they were on welfare. The poverty rate for single women with children fell from 42 percent in 1996 to 34 percent in 2002; before 1996, it had never in recorded history been below 40 percent. This was the first boom ever where poverty declined faster for that group than for married-couple families. Nor did leavers disdain their "dead-end jobs." Studies consistently found that ex-recipients who went on to become waitresses, grill cooks, and security guards took pride in being salarywomen.

Still, it's fair to say that while post-reform America did not look like Calcutta, it was no low-wage worker's paradise, either, especially as the economy weakened in late 2001. Ex–welfare mothers were still poorer than single mothers overall. Some who worked had less income than on welfare. Many were not working full-time, and an estimated 40 percent of those who left the welfare rolls returned later on. In 1999, close to 10 percent of leavers were "disconnected"—neither working nor on welfare nor supported by a working spouse. By the recession year of 2002, that number had risen to almost 14 percent. From the beginning, studies from the Children's Defense Fund and the Center for Budget and Policy Priorities warned of an increase in the number of families in deep poverty, and a steady stream of rumors claimed that soup kitchens and homeless shelters had crowds of ex-recipients clamoring at their doors.

But at least some of these warnings turned out to have been yet more crying wolf. Those who returned to the dole tended soon to find other means of support, getting a new job, signing up for disability or unemployment insurance, or turning to employed partners. As for deepening poverty, experts are often unsure what to make of official estimates of the income of the poorest of the poor, since they may have other sources of support than reported income. So they try to see if the income numbers conform to other measures. There was no evidence that single mothers were moving in with relatives, as you might expect if money were that tight. Harvard researchers Christopher Jencks and Scott Winship, neither of them avid reform supporters, found that, despite a big drop in the number of families using food stamps, worry among single mothers and kids about being able to afford the next meal declined between 1995 and 2000, and though such insecurity increased in the early 2000s, it never rose to pre-reform levels. Moreover, the lowest earners were buying more—spending money that, according to official numbers, they didn't have.

And that takes us to concern number three—the kids. Children were the unreformed's most lethal weapon: the image of kids starving in the streets, sleeping on grates, begging from strangers, and neglected and abused by desperate mothers, was enough to make the most robust reformer queasy. But the predicted Dickensian purgatory also turned out to be wrong. There may have been an increase in the number of children in foster care, but child abuse and neglect numbers are, depending on what measures you use, either unchanged or down.

More striking was what happened to rates of child poverty. They not only went down; by 2001, they hit all-time lows for black children. And though the numbers drifted up again during the recession, they were still lower than they had been pre-reform. On other measures, the young kids of ex–welfare moms are no worse off than under the old regime. Though some studies find lower achievement and more problem behavior among adolescents, the big picture doesn't show teen children in more trouble post-reform. After 1996, juvenile violence and teen pregnancy continued to go down, as they had since the early nineties.

As for the anti-reformer's final concern—the states' "race to the bottom"—that dog didn't bark, either. True, the enemies of reform might point at the 20-odd states that introduced a "family cap," which sought to stem illegitimacy by denying any increase in benefits to women who had another child while on welfare, and whose efficacy remains uncertain. But there's little question that the unreformed were wrong here as well—for the fourth time. The states were, if anything, *nicer* than the feds. No state barred cash benefits to teen mothers, though TANF permitted them to do so. Forty-seven states made it easier than the old system for leavers to keep some of their cash benefits when they first went to work. Many states, including New York, did away with TANF's five-year time limit for all intents and purposes by using state dollars to pick up the tab for those still on the dole at the time and deemed unable to work.

As caseloads declined, the states moved the federal money they would have spent on welfare benefits into work support—transportation, child care, and the like. In fact, under the states' management, welfare has morphed into an unprecedentedly generous work-support program. The real proof that the states were not the scoundrels that opponents had warned they would be came as Congress debated reauthorization after TANF expired in 2002. Reformers argued for even stricter federally mandated work requirements, while those who once warned that the states would engage in a race to the bottom demanded more state control.

This, then, is where we find ourselves today, ten years after reform: a record number of poor single mothers off the dole and the majority of them gainfully employed; less poverty among single mothers, especially black single mothers, as well as their kids; children adjusting well enough; and state governments taking care of their own. The situation is so far from what experts predicted that, as New York University political scientist Lawrence Mead has put it, it brings to mind the Sovietologists at the fall of the Soviet Union.

[...]

Chapter 2

Is Word-Gap Theory a Solution to the Poverty Cycle?

Empowering Underprivileged Children Through Education

Maya Shankar

Maya Shankar, PhD, serves as a senior advisor at the White House Office of Science and Technology Policy.

During the first years of life, a poor child hears roughly 30 million fewer total words than her more affluent peers. Children who experience this drought in heard words have vocabularies that are half the size of their peers by age 3, putting them at a disadvantage before they even step foot in a classroom.

Research shows that during the first years of life, a poor child hears roughly 30 million fewer total words than her more affluent peers. Critically, what she *hears* has direct consequences for what she *learns*. Children who experience this drought in heard words have vocabularies that are half the size of their peers by age 3, putting them at a disadvantage before they even step foot in a classroom.

This is what we call the "word gap," and it can lead to disparities not just in vocabulary size, but also in school readiness, long-term educational and health outcomes, earnings, and family stability even decades later.

It's important to note that talking to one's baby doesn't just promote language development. It promotes *brain development* more broadly. Every time a parent or caregiver has a positive, engaging verbal interaction with a baby – whether it's talking, singing, or reading – neural connections of all kinds are strengthened within the baby's rapidly growing brain.

That's why today we are releasing a new video message from President Obama focused on the importance of supporting learning in our youngest children to help bridge the word gap and improve their chances for later success in school and in life. The President's message builds on the key components of his Early Learning Initiative, which proposes a comprehensive plan to provide high-quality early education to children from birth to school entry.

The President's message is part of a week-long campaign organized in partnership with Too Small to Fail, a joint initiative of the Bill, Hillary & Chelsea Clinton Foundation and Next Generation, to raise awareness of the importance of closing the word gap. The video series follows the first-ever White House Summit on Working Families that explored innovative solutions to help expand opportunities for working families and businesses. The Summit explored a wide range of issues, including expanding access to affordable child care and early education opportunities for families.

Our children's future is so important, bipartisan leaders are all doing their part to help close the word gap. Watch messages from former Secretary of State Hillary Clinton, former Senate Majority Leader Bill Frist, and Cindy McCain, and share these messages with your networks to help spread the word about this cause.

This fall, the White House Office of Science and Technology Policy and the Department of Health and Human Services will team up with Too Small to Fail and the Urban Institute to host an event designed to increase public understanding and make progress on this important issue. This event will highlight initiatives across the country focused on bridging the word gap, including:

- Too Small to Fail's *Talking is Teaching* public action campaign aimed at educating parents about the importance of talking to one's baby and testing out community-level approaches, including in Tulsa, Oklahoma, where Too Small to Fail is working in partnership with the George Kaiser Family Foundation. This campaign will engage pediatricians, business owners, faith-based leaders, librarians, and others to share with parents and caregivers how simple actions (e.g., describing objects seen during a walk or bus ride, singing songs, or telling stories) can significantly improve a baby's ability to learn new words and concepts.

- Georgia's *Talk with Me Baby*, a scalable, public action strategy aimed at increasing early exposure to language and public understanding of the primacy of language. This program provides professional development to nurses, the nation's largest healthcare workforce, who will coach new and expectant parents to deliver "language nutrition" to their kids. With funding from the Greater United Way of Atlanta, this collaborative effort brings together the Georgia Department of Public Health and Department of Education, Emory University's Nell Hodgson Woodruff School of Nursing, and Georgia Tech.

- The City of Providence's *Providence Talks*, which provides members of the Providence community, where two-thirds of kindergarteners enroll below national literacy standards, with home-based caregiver coaching interventions. These interventions harness innovative technologies from the LENA Foundation, including word "pedometers" that record and provide quantitative feedback to caregivers on the number of words spoken and the number of conversations had with children. Providence Talks is hosted by Mayor Taveras of Providence, Rhode Island, and is supported by the Bloomberg Foundation.

- The University of Chicago, School of Medicine's *Thirty Million Words® Initiative* with its tiered intervention approach to optimizing caregiver-child talk at the individual, community, and population levels. Researchers recently received funds from the PNC Foundation to support a five-year longitudinal study of the program's impact.

Children Perform Better When Parents Are More Involved

Rachel Williams

Rachel Williams is a freelance feature writer with the Guardian. *She has also been published in* HuffPost, Refinery29, *and* Daily Mail.

Middle-class pupils do better because parents and schools put more effort into their education, according to a study published today.

Researchers found that children from poorer backgrounds were not predisposed to work less hard, but parents' attitudes were most important, making more of a difference than schools themselves.

But schools also put more effort in with pupils from better-off homes, perhaps because of the pressure exerted by pushy middle-class parents, the team from the universities of Leicester and Leeds said.

They said the findings suggested that policies aimed at improving parental effort could be effective in increasing children's educational attainment.

The research, Must Try Harder, used the National Child Development Study, which follows individuals born in a given week in 1958 throughout their lives.

Effort was measured using indicators of a student's attitude, such as the answers given by 16-year-olds to questions including whether they think school is a "waste of time", and teachers' views about students' laziness.

Other factors studied were the parents' interest in their children's education, measured by, for example, whether they read to their children or attended meetings with teachers.

Variables studied for schools in the research, which is published in the Review of Economics and Statistics, included the extent of parental involvement initiated by the school and whether 16-year-olds were offered career guidance.

Professor Gianni De Fraja, head of economics at Leicester, said: "Parents from a more advantaged environment exert more effort, and this influences positively the educational attainment of their children.

"The parents' background also increases the school's effort, which increases the school achievement. Why schools work harder where parents are from a more privileged background we do not know. It might be because middle-class parents are more vocal in demanding that the school work hard. Influencing parental effort is certainly something that is much easier than modifying their social background."

A separate study, commissioned by the then Department for Children, Schools and Families, and released on Wednesday, found that modern languages were compulsory for 14-year-olds in fewer than a fifth of English schools last year, with the numbers much lower among schools with the highest number of pupils from poor backgrounds.

Researchers found that studying a language at GCSE was merely optional at more than two thirds (69%) of the 1,100 schools surveyed. At 11%, languages were compulsory for some but not all, and at 18% they were compulsory for no one.

At higher-achieving schools and those with low proportions of pupils on free school meals, languages were more likely to be compulsory.

Among those in the 20% with the highest numbers of children getting free meals, fewer than one in 10 ruled that pupils had to take a language at GCSE. In schools in the 20% with the lowest numbers on free meals, the figure was more than 50%.

Talk Is Vital to a Child's Brain Development

Cory Turner

Cory Turner edits and reports for the NPR Ed *team.*

It's not just baby talk. Any kind of talk with young children — especially if they're too young to talk back — will do.

Because talk is vital to a child's brain development, says Dana Suskind, who found her passion for literacy in an unlikely place: the operating room.

As a surgeon, Suskind performed cochlear implants at the University of Chicago. The implant is a remarkable marriage of medicine and technology that can help even profoundly deaf children hear. But Suskind noticed that her young patients went on to develop language skills at wildly different rates. Some reached or surpassed grade level. Some didn't. Why?

In Suskind's new book, *Thirty Million Words: Building A Child's Brain*, she explains her personal journey toward the surprising answer: The kids who thrived generally lived in households where they heard lots of words. Millions and millions of words.

The kids who received cochlear implants but struggled to develop language often did so because their parents didn't talk to them as much as their growing brains required. Suskind writes, "without that language environment, the ability to hear is a wasted gift." And so the surgeon became an activist. For talk.

I spoke with Suskind about that journey and her Thirty Million Words Initiative.

Can you explain what you mean when you talk about the 30 million word gap?

The 30 million word gap comes from a very famous study that was done probably about 30 years ago by Betty Hart and

Todd Risley, where they followed a group of children between 0 and 3 years old from all socioeconomic backgrounds. And basically what they found, by the end of age 3, children from low-socioeconomic backgrounds will have heard 30 million fewer words than their more affluent peers. And this number itself was correlated not just with differences in vocabulary but also differences in IQ and test scores in the third grade.

Why does it seem so closely correlated with parents' socioeconomic status?

The reasons are multi-faceted. Certainly background — how you were raised. In some families it's prized to be seen and not heard, especially in some low-income families. Number two, the stressors of poverty can't be underestimated. If you have unstable jobs or child care or home life, certainly that's going to impact your bandwidth for talking. But there's another important area that we're really focusing on: this idea that many families haven't been exposed to the powerful science that shows that their language is the key architect for their children's brain growth. Our focus is empowering parents with that knowledge.

What was new to me and really alarming was the difference in tone — in the nature of the words that kids heard. According to Hart and Risley, the children of "professional" parents heard six times as many positive phrases (in one year) compared with the children of "welfare" parents ...

The most stark findings of Hart and Risley were really the differences in affirmations versus prohibitions. The difference between "get down, don't do that" versus explaining "we need to pick up these blocks because we're going to go out and play." There was a huge difference along socioeconomic lines. Not only does that impact children's language development, but it can often be related to toxic stress which impacts children's ability to learn as well as their own view of themselves. And we say, you know, if you spend your life — from home to school and into society — hearing over and over again that you're not good enough, that's certainly going to impact you to your core.

What's happening in the brain from ages 0 to 3 when parents really need to be talking to their kids? Why is talk at this age so important?

In the first three years of life, you'll have no more rapid and robust brain growth than during that time. It's when 80 to 85 percent of the physical brain develops. We're all born with 100 billion neurons, but those neurons are meaningless without those connections. And what results in those connections? It's really about parent talk and interaction.

The brain, unlike any other organ, is pretty unformed when you're born, and it's completely dependent on this environmental input: parent talk. So that's why, in your first three years of life, you're basically building the foundation for all your thinking and learning through parent talk and interaction. ... Because hearing is not really about the ear but the brain's process. And, as the child gets older, the brain begins to prune away connections that are not used as much. And what happens is, if it hasn't heard sound, it starts pruning away those important connections.

Why is it that most of the money that federal, state and local governments spend to reduce the achievement gap is spent after kids leave this precious 0-to-3 period?

[At that age] we're talking about the family's and community's impact on a child's brain growth and academic trajectory. So it's a little more difficult to think about how to approach it. And [governments] have much more control when kids are in school. That being said, unless we truly understand the science and address this 0-to-3 issue, we will never be able to truly start moving the needle on this achievement gap. We have to reconcile the fact that we're going to have to rethink how we approach education in order to get the results that we want.

With your Thirty Million Words Initiative, how do you propose doing that?

We're really trying to take on this idea that, if early language environments — basically how and how much parents and caregivers talk and interact with their children — is fundamental to brain growth, then we want to see really a population-level shift. So that every parent, every caregiver, every educator, every policymaker understands how powerful language is in allowing every child to reach their genetic, intellectual potential. So we are developing science-based programs that really meet families where they are. We're working on a maternity ward intervention where new mothers and fathers learn about the power of language. We're working in pediatricians' offices, home-visiting programs as well as children's museums and libraries. Our program is about getting this message and these science-based programs to parents — to really, hopefully, get it into the groundwater.

What do you think it's going to take to make this a household idea: that kids need to hear a lot of words and they need to hear them early?

One of my favorite parts of our program is called "Spread the Words." It's about parents becoming the agents of change within their communities. We not only translate the science so they can understand it and work with their children, but they become — I don't want to say evangelists, but agents of change. So they actively spread the words, and we trace out their social networks. And I tell you there is nothing more powerful than for a parent to understand how powerful they are.

There's one simple, little prescription that seems to be at the heart of your program. Can you walk me through what you call the Three T's?

Yeah, the first T is "Tune In." Really tuning into what your child's interested in, following his or her lead, or getting him or her interested in what you're doing. The second is "Talk More," which is really just talking using rich vocabulary, talking about the past and future. Lastly is "Taking Turns." Really viewing your child as a conversational partner from Day One. So many parents don't realize that, even before a child's first word, they are practicing how to have a conversation. So if you respond to every coo or babble, you are starting to help build that ability. ... Until I started doing this research, I think I looked at parent-child interaction as a throwaway. But when you actually look at it, in the going back and forth, you can almost see the neurons in the baby's brain developing as you're taking turns in the social dance, if you will.

One City's Success Story with Closing the Word-Gap

Elizabeth Mann Levesque

Elizabeth Mann Levesque is a fellow at the Brown Center on Education Policy at Brookings. She studies how institutional constraints shape the policymaking process and policy design, with a focus on K–12 education policy.

Two decades ago, researchers Betty Hart and Todd Risley revealed a particularly stark difference in the experiences of toddlers with different income levels. As Hart and Risley described it, low-income infants hear many fewer words per day than their middle- and high-income peers, totaling to a 30-million-word difference by age three. They coined this discrepancy "the word gap." Hart and Risley also found that students who had heard fewer words as toddlers correlated with worse performance on tests of vocabulary and language development years later.

More recent studies have similarly identified a word gap, albeit not to the tune of 30 million words, and shown that spoken word counts predicted vocabulary and language understanding months later even when controlling for previous vocabulary levels and maternal education. A separate study showed that, by age two, toddlers from lower socio-economic backgrounds can be six months behind their wealthier peers in vocabulary. Despite widespread acknowledgement of the scale of the problem, including a push from former President Barack Obama on the issue, progress toward closing the word gap has been slow.

Providence Talks Implementation and Results

A number of cities have begun addressing this problem with innovative programs. In the 2013 Mayors Challenge, Bloomberg

"The 'word gap' and 1 city's plan to close it," by Elizabeth Mann Levesque, The Brookings Institution, July 10, 2017. Reprinted by permission.

Philanthropies awarded the grand prize and a $5 million grant to the city of Providence, R.I., for an innovative plan to reduce this word gap. In May, four years after the competition, Bloomberg released preliminary results of the program.

Though a small city with fewer than 200,000 residents, Providence faces challenges that are common across larger urban areas. In 2013, when the city won the Mayors Challenge, 85 percent of Providence Public School District students were eligible for free or reduced-price lunch, and only 66 percent of students graduated high school in four years. Barely 30 percent of students entering kindergarten demonstrated benchmark early literacy skills. To the extent that Providence is successful in minimizing the word gap, its efforts could be informative for cities across the United States.

Providence's program–titled Providence Talks–relied on a recording device called a "word pedometer" to monitor and improve spoken word counts in low-income homes. The program originally paired families with in-home coaches to analyze the data from the pedometer, and as the program scaled up to its peak of more than 1,300 toddlers, Providence Talks adopted other structures as well. For example, the family playgroup model facilitated conversations between parents about child development and strategies to increase engagement with children, while the leader analyzed each family's recordings with the adults before or afterwards. Every visit, in the home or to a playgroup, included a free book for families to keep.

The word pedometer tracked both words spoken and conversational turns–the number of times the conversation changes from an adult to a child and back again, roughly a measure of the give and take in a conversation. The device, designed by Colorado-based LENA, was placed in a small pocket in a special toddler vest and could record words spoken in Spanish and English. It recorded all words in a child's environment and can separate words spoken by an adult from television or other noises.

Bloomberg Philanthropies reported this May that 60 percent of children in Providence Talks heard more words at the end of the program than at the beginning. On average, the number of words toddlers heard in a day increased by 50 percent. Families who started at the lowest end of the spectrum, whose children heard fewer than 8,000 words a day at the outset—barely more than half of the 15,000 words needed for healthy brain development–recorded strong gains of 45 percent in words recorded. Ninety-seven percent of parents reported being satisfied or highly satisfied with the program.

Providence Talks has partnered with Brown University researchers to examine the effects of the increase in spoken words on the toddlers' language skills. In a city with 40 percent child poverty, eight percentage points higher than the national average, these changes and the program that produced them could have the potential to shrink developmental gaps long-term.

Date Limitations

Notably, the word pedometer used by Providence Talks does not measure the complexity of the words spoken nor their tone. "The soup is very hot" counts the same as "the computer mouse is broken," even though the second sentence includes more difficult vocabulary. However, recent research indicates that quality may matter more than the quantity itself. Similarly, "Do not touch that!" counts the same as "I'm proud of you," although research that indicates affirmations build confidence and skills better than prohibitions.

While Providence Talks coaches work individually with families to build quality and affirmations into daily word counts, the word pedometer does not track this progress, and researchers are unable to listen to the audio themselves. The Rhode Island branch of the American Civil Liberties Union, concerned with privacy issues at the outset of the program, convinced Providence Talks to implement automatic deletion of the files after analysis by a computer.

Moving Forward

Despite these limitations, the initial success of Providence Talks suggests a potential strategy for closing the word gap. Some organizations and cities have already begun to replicate this work, including the Talking is Teaching initiative by the Clinton Foundation and The Opportunity Institute, to raise awareness of the word gap and conversational strategies to boost word use with children. A Georgia program called Talk with Me Baby premiered in 2013 to discuss the importance of talking to children with their parents. In Hartford, Conn., a community agency has started a program called Words Count to improve language skills of children under 5 years old through weekly home visits and word pedometers, an initiative similar to the Providence program. The Thirty Million Words Initiative at the University of Chicago plans a community-based rollout of their language-focused curriculum this year.

Measures of school readiness–such as the ability to recognize all the letters, write one's name, and count to 20–have reflected substantial differences between low-income students and their wealthier peers for decades. The aforementioned research has shown that these differences originate early and persist, making the word gap a promising target for intervention. Building on the success of Providence Talks, other cities could similarly target the word gap to leverage the power of the home in early childhood education.

Word-Gap Is Based on Groundless Evidence

Leah Durán

Leah Durán is an assistant professor at the University of Arizona.

Almost without exception, articles about early education begin by referencing the word gap, citing it as one of the most important problems in early education and a major factor in educational inequity. The study that proposed the notion of a word gap has received extensive media coverage, making its way across the country and even to the White House. Many well-meaning programs and policies are now built on the premise that children from low-income households enter school with less-developed language skills than children from wealthier ones, and that if poor parents talked more or in "better" ways to their children, their children would do better in school. Despite being referenced over and over again as an established fact, the notion of a word gap is built on shaky evidence.

For research in any field, any one study is just a single data point, and this one is particularly weak. The "30 million words" study by researchers Hart and Risley has been widely critiqued by peers as methodologically flawed. In addition to making claims about all poor families based on six families in Kansas, the researchers made highly subjective judgments about what counts as "high quality" or "low quality" language, and did not account for the way that being observed changes people's behavior.

The researchers also found no significant causal relationship between the number of words they counted and children's academic outcomes. But popular media articles repeatedly point to this study as proof that a word gap is one of the primary causes of educational struggles in low-income schools and communities.

"The Truth About the Word Gap," by Leah Durán, OZY, February 20, 2017. Reprinted by permission.

Yet there is a deep body of research in linguistics, sociolinguistics and linguistic anthropology, and education that directly contradicts the notion that there is a "language gap" or that poor children are linguistically disadvantaged. Sociolinguist William Labov, for one, spent most of his career studying language use in low-income African-American communities, and described children in such families as "bathed in verbal stimulation from morning to night."

This kind of research rarely makes it into the media. Instead, we read over and over again in the newspaper that poor children do poorly in school because they don't have enough language, or the right kind of language. The word gap theory is so troubling not only because it's probably incorrect but also because the proposed remedies are counterproductive.

In a well-intentioned initiative, parents were provided with "word pedometers" to track the number of words they said, as well as coaching on how to improve their language. This word counting is a simplistic understanding of language and likely a waste of money. There is no evidence that if poor parents say more words to their children, those children will do better in school. But anti-poverty measures have demonstrated meaningful and lasting effects on children's educational outcomes.

Between 1994 and 1998, the New Hope Project in Milwaukee, Wisconsin, for example, showed that modestly supplementing poor parents' incomes led to long-term improvements in their children's educational outcomes. If the real problem is poverty, why not alleviate poverty? Poverty, after all, presents real challenges to children's learning, such as food insecurity. Parents who need to work two or three jobs to stay afloat have less time to spend with their children, and less money to spend on things like books or tutoring.

Schools that serve low-income communities are usually under-resourced, and money does matter in efforts to improve educational outcomes in these schools. But headlines suggesting that the most powerful thing we can do for poor kids is "completely free" implies that some people see the idea of a word gap as absolving districts and policymakers of the obligation to invest real money in solutions to address educational inequity. Instead, belief in a word gap transfers responsibility for the problem to parents, and away from legislators.

Moreover, some teachers interpret the idea of a word gap to mean that their students are not capable of challenging intellectual work. In a self-fulfilling prophecy, those who see their students as less capable tend to offer them fewer opportunities to learn.

As a teacher educator, it is my responsibility to help future teachers understand how to provide engaging, meaningful and rigorous education to all children, including those living in poverty. Lately, this has involved asking teachers to reconsider some of the "commonsense" ideas about language that they have already heard. I ask you to do the same.

Word-Gap Theory Is Culturally Offensive

Gulnaz Saiyed and Natalia Smirnov

Gulnaz Saiyed and Natalia Smirnov are doctoral candidates in the Learning Sciences Group at Northwestern University's School of Education and Social Policy.

The American public are aware of our many gaps: The wealth gap in the U.S. is worse than in most industrialized nations; we have a skills gap, with American students falling behind the rest of the world on science and math exams; and the achievement gap between white, black and Latino students continues to be an embarrassment and driver of education reform.

Now comes the 30 million-word gap, which is gaining traction in education, research — and political circles.

According to the Clinton Foundation, the word gap is too big to ignore and "too small to fail." This gap — also known as "language gap" or "vocabulary gap" — is based on a two-decades-old research finding that children from "welfare" families were exposed to an average of 30 million fewer words than children from high-income families during their first four years.

Education reformers and policymakers have mobilized to close the 30 million-word gap, convinced that parents should have more conversations with their children in order to head off the deficits in schooling and income that persist for the poor and minorities as they grow up.

This, in turn, has spurred large-scale university-led interventions such as the University of Chicago-based "Thirty Million Words Initiative" to get parents to talk more to their kids.

Meanwhile, Hillary Clinton has fastened on the word gap as a key education reform plank in her expected run for the presidency in 2016. "Coming to school without words is like coming to school

"Does '30 Million-Word Gap' Have Gap in Authenticity?" By Gulnaz Saiyed and Natalia Smirnov, Youth Project and Youth Today, January 20, 2015. Reprinted by permission.

without food or adequate health care," she wrote in an October 2014 Clinton Foundation commentary.

But pinning the differences in school achievement and adult income on the number of words heard by the age of 3 is overly narrow and strategically unsound.

The word gap rhetoric plays on the pair of values dear to the American ethos: diversity and meritocracy — the idea that anyone, no matter his or her background, can be successful. However, by presenting white and wealthy parenting practices as a singular pathway to success, the Word Gap movement essentially casts our supposedly valued diversity as a deficit.

This latest "big idea" isn't new. It was spawned in 1995 when two researchers at the University of Kansas, Betty Hart and Todd Risley, observed parents interacting with their child for one hour a month for 2 1/2 years, then multiplied their data to account for the times they weren't around. Let's see what's wrong with their research and this newest solution to America's problems.

First, arithmetic sleight-of-hand. If 30 million words sounds far too big a difference, that's because it is. This number was calculated by comparing the parent and child talk word output of six African-American welfare families against 13 — that's 13 — upper-middle class and mostly white families.

Second, ethnic and cultural bias. They didn't include Latinos, Asians and nontraditional family configurations.

And third, skimpy observations. Their study didn't include words and sounds heard during play among siblings or overheard from adult talking or nonverbal communication.

No wonder the 30 million-word disparity.

But despite the limits of this original study, other researchers readily tied the word gap to children's brain development and early literacy skills, rhetorically linking the school-based achievement gap to differences in language exposure that begin before children even start school.

Politicians have added their voices. In an online post Clinton said of the word gap that it "leads to further disparities in achievement and success over time, from academic performance and persistence to earnings and family stability even 20 and 30 years later."

We support the Clinton Foundation and other similar organizations' focus on early learning and low-income families. However, the strategy of intervening into parents' vocabulary and speech patterns in particular is being presented as a cure-all for much greater systemic inequalities.

Missing from Clinton's pipeline-to-adult failure argument are institutional disadvantages that parents *don't* control, such as inequitable school funding, biases in standardized tests and the effort spent to navigate life in poverty while wealthier families cultivate internship opportunities and academic tutoring for their children.

In effect, the word gap interventions propose that improving social and economic outcomes for poor and minority families can be as simple as training them to act more white and middle-class (and monitoring their compliance with a "word pedometer"). Policymakers and researchers suggest that parents who don't talk with their children this way are missing out on a simple, easy, obvious and research-supported method for success.

But a long tradition of learning sciences research complicates that claim. Consider: What if we assumed that all parents, whatever their background, want the best for their kids and are making different choices for their children given their own circumstances? Studies show that Chinese-American mothers use approaches that socialize children into cultural values of family and community.

This includes teaching children to observe more than talk. And some African-American parents raise their boys not to talk too much, because this might be perceived as disruptive in schools. So while Hart and Risley found that some children hear fewer words than others, they did not ask why that might be the case.

The two also suggest that students who hear more words enter kindergarten with larger vocabularies, which in turn helps them succeed in school. But they only measure the children's knowledge of Standard English, using the culturally biased Peabody Vocabulary test.

Further, other research shows that a reason middle-class children do better in school on average is because typical middle-class parenting includes verbal interactions that mirror what children hear in school ("What does the cow say?" "Moo-moo!" "Yes, that's right!"). Some children are simply not raised with adults asking them questions with obvious answers.

While middle-class activities do lead children to develop a sense of entitlement, individuality and set them up to feel comfortable in schools, they de-emphasize other childhood experiences. For example, many working-class parents do not overschedule their children with extracurricular activities. Instead, they provide opportunities for play, development of curiosity, creativity and respect for different perspectives.

These are qualities we know are important for an innovative economy.

Additionally, children from different backgrounds come to school with different skill sets. Bilingual students have been shown to outperform their monolingual peers on measures of self-control, and bilingualism has long-term cognitive, social and socioemotional benefits. Children who speak African American English Vernacular (AAEV) have a rich and deep understanding of language and wordplay, which can be used in classrooms as a bridge to academic literary analysis.

The examples above illustrate that differences are not deficits. Culturally diverse environments often provide children with richly diverse social and cognitive toolkits, which should be developed and expanded upon in school. This is because we know they are valuable in the real world. Examples of culturally relevant education are shown to lead to positive academic and social outcomes. But, there is no study directly linking vocabulary size to long-term school achievement.

The writers of the Clinton Foundation report, "Too Small to Fail," argue that the poverty of vocabulary should be discussed with the same passion as child hunger. They say we should be outraged and moved to action by the parents who fail to feed their children with words.

We say that a focus on early vocabulary exposure as the key and mitigating factor that produces different long-term outcomes between children is narrow and unproductive.

To be sure, we should enact research-based policies to support parents to feed their children with words, with experiences, with skills and knowledge. But spending our money promoting just one (white, middle class) way of doing that, and just in the first few years of a child's life, is nearsighted and cripples diversity.

We should instead focus our resources on culturally relevant programs that build a broad range of literacy, cognitive and social skills over time, and not just limited to early childhood. These could include vocabulary interventions, but they should not be limited to them if we genuinely believe in building an egalitarian, pluralistic society in which we make the most of human potential — including individual and cultural differences — to feed conversation, creativity and innovation.

Music Is Another Way to Help Improve Kids' Language

Cory Turner

Cory Turner edits and reports for the NPR Ed *team.*

Musical training doesn't just improve your ear for music — it also helps your ear for speech. That's the takeaway from an unusual new study published in *The Journal of Neuroscience*. Researchers found that kids who took music lessons for two years didn't just get better at playing the trombone or violin; they found that playing music also helped kids› brains process language.

And here's something else unusual about the study: where it took place. It wasn't a laboratory, but in the offices of Harmony Project in Los Angeles. It's a nonprofit after-school program that teaches music to children in low-income communities.

Two nights a week, neuroscience and musical learning meet at Harmony's Hollywood headquarters, where some two-dozen children gather to learn how to play flutes, oboes, trombones and trumpets. The program also includes on-site instruction at many public schools across Los Angeles County.

Harmony Project is the brainchild of Margaret Martin, whose life path includes parenting two kids while homeless before earning a doctorate in public health. A few years ago, she noticed something remarkable about the kids who had gone through her program.

"Since 2008, 93 percent of our high school seniors have graduated in four years and have gone on to colleges like Dartmouth, Tulane, NYU," Martin says, "despite dropout rates of 50 percent or more in the neighborhoods where they live and where we intentionally site our programs."

There are plenty of possible explanations for that success. Some of the kids and parents the program attracts are clearly driven. Then there's access to instruments the kids couldn't otherwise afford, and the lessons, of course. Perhaps more importantly, Harmony Project gives kids a place to go after the bell rings, and access to adults who will challenge and nurture them. Keep in mind, many of these students come from families or neighborhoods that have been ravaged by substance abuse or violence — or both.

Still, Martin suspected there was something else, too — something about actually playing music — that was helping these kids.

Enter neurobiologist Nina Kraus, who runs the Auditory Neuroscience Laboratory at Northwestern University. When a mutual acquaintance at the National Institutes of Health introduced her to Martin, Kraus jumped at the chance to explore Martin's hunch and to study the Harmony Project kids and their brains.

Breaking Down Brainwaves

Before we get to what, exactly, Kraus' team did or how they did it, here's a quick primer on how the brain works:

The brain depends on neurons. Whenever we take in new information — through our ears, eyes or skin — those neurons talk to each other by firing off electrical pulses. We call these brainwaves. With scalp electrodes, Kraus and her team can both see and hear these brainwaves.

Using some relatively new, expensive and complicated technology, Kraus can also break these brainwaves down into their component parts — to better understand how kids process not only music but speech, too. That's because the two aren't that different. They have three common denominators — pitch, timing and timbre — and the brain uses the same circuitry to make sense of them all.

In other research, Kraus had noticed something about the brains of kids who come from poverty, like many in the Harmony

Project. These children often hear fewer words by age 5 than other kids do.

And that's a problem, Kraus says, because "in the absence of stimulation, the nervous system ... hungry for stimulation ... will make things up. So, in the absence of sound, what we saw is that there was just more random background activity, which you might think of as static."

In addition to that "neural noise," as Kraus calls it, ability to process sound — like telling the difference between someone saying "ba" and "ga" — requires microsecond precision in the brain. And many kids raised in poverty, Kraus says, simply have a harder time doing it; individual sounds can seem "blurry" to the brain.

Working with Harmony Project, Kraus randomly assigned several dozen kids from the program's waitlist into two groups: those who would be studied after one year of music lessons and those who would be studied after two years.

And what she found was that in the two-year kids, the static didn't go away. But their brains got better — more precise — at processing sound. In short: less blur.

Why the Improvement?

It goes back to pitch, timing and timbre. Kraus argues that learning music improves the brain's ability to process all three, which helps kids pick up language, too. Consonants and vowels become clearer, and the brain can make sense of them more quickly.

That's also likely to make life easier at school, not just in music class but in math class, too — and everywhere else.

To be clear, the study has its limits. It was small — roughly 50 kids, ranging in age from 6 to 9. It wasn't conducted in a lab. And it's hard to know if kids doing some other activity could have experienced similar benefits.

But 10th-grader Monica Miranda doesn't need proof that playing violin has helped her. She's one of the first students in the door at a recent Harmony Project re-enrollment event in the auditorium of a nearby elementary school.

"I feel like music really connects with education," she says. "It helps you concentrate more."

Miranda is in her third year with Harmony Project.

"When I do my homework or I'm studying for something and I feel overwhelmed, I usually go to my violin, to start playing it," Miranda says. "I feel like it relaxes my mind. And coming here to play with an orchestra, it's just amazing. I love it."

And, the science says, her brain loves it, too.

Low-Income Students Need Better School Funding, Not a Better Vocabulary

US Department of Education

The US Department of Education is a federal agency whose mission is to promote student achievement and preparation for global competitiveness by fostering educational excellence and ensuring equal access.

A new report from the U.S. Department of Education documents that schools serving low-income students are being shortchanged because school districts across the country are inequitably distributing their state and local funds.

The analysis of new data on 2008-09 school-level expenditures shows that many high-poverty schools receive less than their fair share of state and local funding, leaving students in high-poverty schools with fewer resources than schools attended by their wealthier peers.

The data reveal that more than 40 percent of schools that receive federal Title I money to serve disadvantaged students spent less state and local money on teachers and other personnel than schools that don't receive Title I money at the same grade level in the same district.

"Educators across the country understand that low-income students need extra support and resources to succeed, but in far too many places policies for assigning teachers and allocating resources are perpetuating the problem rather than solving it," said U.S. Secretary of Education Arne Duncan said. "The good news in this report is that it is feasible for districts to address this problem and it will have a significant impact on educational opportunities for our nation's poorest children."

"More Than 40% of Low-Income Schools Don't Get a Fair Share of State and Local Funds, Department of Education Research Finds," U.S. Department of Education, November 30, 2011.

In a policy brief that accompanies the report, a Department analysis found that providing low-income schools with comparable spending would cost as little as 1 percent of the average district's total spending. The analysis also found that extra resources would make a big impact by adding as much as between 4 percent and 15 percent to the budget of schools serving high numbers of students who live in poverty.

The Title I program is designed to provide extra resources to high-poverty schools to help them meet the greater challenges of educating at-risk students. The law includes a requirement that districts ensure that Title I schools receive "comparability of services" from state and local funds, so that federal funds can serve their intended purpose of supplementing equitable state and local funding.

In recent years a growing number of researchers, education advocates, and legislators have highlighted that by not requiring districts to consider actual school-level expenditures in calculating "comparability of services," the existing comparability requirement doesn't address fundamental spending inequities within districts. Instead, districts can show comparability in a number of easier ways, such as by using a districtwide salary schedule. This masks the fact that schools serving disadvantaged students often have less experienced teachers who are paid less. It also undermines the purpose of Title I funding, as districts can use federal funds to fill state and local funding gaps instead of providing additional services to students in poverty.

For the study, Education Department researchers analyzed new school-level spending and teacher salary data submitted by more than 13,000 school districts as required by the American Recovery and Reinvestment Act (ARRA) of 2009. This school level expenditure data was made available for the first time ever in this data collection.

Using the data from the ARRA collection, Department staff analyzed the impact and feasibility of making this change to Title I comparability. That policy brief finds that:

- Fixing the comparability provision is feasible. As many as 28 percent of Title I districts would be out of compliance with reformed comparability provisions. But compliance for those districts is not as costly as some might think—fixing it would cost only 1 percent to 4 percent of their total school-level expenditures on average.
- Fixing the comparability provision would have a large impact. The benefit to low-spending Title I schools would be significant, as their expenditures would increase by 4 percent to 15 percent. And the low-spending schools that would benefit have much higher poverty rates than other schools in their districts.

Russlynn Ali, assistant secretary for civil rights, said that this analysis shows that closing the comparability loophole is within reach and would provide meaningful help to low-income schools.

"Transparency on resource allocation within school districts is critical to ensuring every child has access to the same educational opportunities. These new data highlight that the Title I comparability provision is broken and has failed to provide access to equitable resources, and that it is possible to fix it."

Under President Obama's Blueprint for Reform of the Elementary and Secondary Education Act, the Title I comparability provision would be revised to ensure that state and local funding levels are distributed equitably between Title I and non-Title I schools. Language to reform Title I comparability is also included in the bill to reauthorize ESEA that the Senate Health, Education, Labor, and Pensions Committee passed last month.

CHAPTER 3

Is Poverty More Closely Related to Behavior than Economics?

The Role of Behavior in Economics

Eshe Nelson

Eshe Nelson is an economics and markets reporter at Quartz *in London, covering everything from the future of finance to inequality.*

Sorry to say it, but you're not perfect. We like to believe that we are smart, rational creatures, always acting in our best interests. In fact, dominant economic theory these days often makes that assumption.

What was left of this illusion was further dismantled by the The Royal Swedish Academy of Sciences, who awarded the Nobel prize in economics to Richard Thaler, an American economist at the University of Chicago, for his pioneering work in behavioral economics, which examines humanity's flaws—namely, why we don't make rational economic decisions.

In 2008, Thaler co-authored the influential book *Nudge: Improving Decisions about Health, Wealth and Happiness* with Cass Sunstein. In this and his other research, Thaler explains the flaws and biases that influence our actions. This led to the theory that you can use subtle nudges to encourage people to make better decisions, particularly when planning for the long term, such as saving for retirement.

Here are some of the main ways behavioral economists like Thaler say we let ourselves down.

Loss Aversion and Anchoring

People can make bad economic choices based on something Thaler dubbed the "endowment effect," which is the theory that people value things more highly when they own them. In other words, you'd ask for more money for selling something that you own than what you would be willing to pay to buy the same thing.

This relates to another key theory, known as loss aversion. People experience the negative feeling of loss more strongly than they feel the positive sense of a gain of the same size. This is also impacted by anchoring: If you are selling an item, your reference point is most likely to be the price you paid for something. Even if the value of that item is now demonstrably worth less, you are anchored to the purchase price, in part because you want to avoid that sense of loss. This can lead to pain in financial markets, in particular.

Planner Versus Doer

We've all been there, torn between making a sensible decision that sets us up well for the future and something that provides more immediate gratification. This is the internal struggle between what Thaler and others describe as your planning self and doing self. One way to avoid this conflict is to remove short-term courses of actions. This goes against the traditional economic notion that more choices are always better.

This is where nudges come in. Thaler and Sunstein pioneered the idea of using nudges to create alternative courses of actions that promote good long-term decision making but maintain freedom of choice. One method of doing this they found is simply changing the default option—switching users from opt-in to opt-out, for example. This has been used in public policy, particularly with the creation of "nudge units" in the US and UK, to boost both retirement savings and organ donation. In 2014, a study by the Economic & Social Research Council found that 51 countries had developed centralized policy units influenced by behavioral sciences.

Availability Heuristic

People are inclined to make decisions based on how readily available information is to them. If you can easily recall something, you are likely to rely more on this information than other facts or observations. This means judgements tend to be heavily weighted on the most recent piece of information received or the simplest thing to recall.

In practice, research has shown that shoppers who can recall a few low-price products—perhaps because of a prominent ads or promotions—tend to think that a store offers low prices across the board, regardless of other evidence. And in a particularly devious experiment, a psychology professor (naturally) got his students to evaluate his teaching, with one group asked to list two things he could improve and another asked to list 10. Since it's harder to think of 10 bad things than just two, the students asked to make a longer list gave the professor *better* ratings—seemingly concluding that if they couldn't come up with enough critical things to fill out the form, then the course must be good.

Status Quo Bias

Most people are likely to stick with the status quo even if there are big gains to be made from a change that involves just a small cost. In particular, this is one of the implications of loss aversion. That's why a nudge, such as changing the default option on a contract, can be so effective. Thaler's research on pension programs shows that while employees can choose to opt-out of a plan, the status quo bias means once they are in it, they are actually more likely to stay put.

Governments have used this to encourage better behavior. In 2006, the US passed a law that encouraged firms to automatically enroll their employees in retirement savings plans, which they could opt out of at any time. By 2011, Thaler and a colleague estimated that 4.1 million people were in some type of automatic escalation plan and annual savings increased by $7.6 billion by 2013. In the UK, a national scheme to automatically enroll people in a personal savings plan had an opt-out rate of just 12%.

These flaws—or human traits, to be more charitable—may not seem unusual, but Thaler argues that appreciating the implications of human behavior has lost its importance in dominant economic theory. As the field relied more and more on mathematics, there was a push to explain the world using rigid, complex economic models. These models tend to focus on what can be measured, and the irrational decisions humans make hardly fits that mold. In a paper last year, Thaler wrote: "It is time stop thinking about behavioral economics as some kind of revolution. Rather, behavioral economics should be considered simply a return to the kind of open-minded, intuitively motivated discipline that was invented by Adam Smith and augmented by increasingly powerful statistical tools and datasets."

Today, behavioral economics is still considered a somewhat separate subject within the broader discipline. But if Thaler has it his way, the field of study that just won him a Nobel prize won't exist for long: "If economics does develop along these lines the term 'behavioral economics' will eventually disappear from our lexicon. All economics will be as behavioral as the topic requires."

Welfare Recipients Need to Spend Money on Food, Not Drugs

Alan Greenblatt

Alan Greenblatt, a reporter at NPR, has been writing about politics and government in Washington and throughout the nation for more than a decade.

Kasha Kelley believes that people on welfare need to spend their money on things like diapers and detergent — not drugs.

Kelley, who has served in the Kansas state House since 2005, sponsored legislation to require a large share of the state's welfare recipients to be tested for drug use, or risk losing their benefits.

"I get a lot of constituents who mention their frustrations with neighbors they know are receiving some sort of public assistance," she says. "They don't feel the money's being used right when they know that drugs are being used in the house, and I would concur with that."

The Kansas House passed Kelley's bill overwhelmingly last year, but it has not won Senate approval. She hasn't given up, though — and neither have legislators in at least nine other states who have introduced similar measures.

It's just common sense, Kelley says. She and other state sponsors of drug testing bills believe that tax dollars should in no way support drug habits. Checking people on public assistance for drugs would not only save money, they argue, but put welfare recipients on firmer footing when they get ready to enter the working world.

Craig P. Blair introduced a similar bill in West Virginia. "The fact is that we have to respect the taxpayer and help the people be work-qualified and be good parents, also," he says.

Designed to Demean?

Critics of these bills say they're not just misguided but unconstitutional. It's already a given in most welfare programs that if a recipient is suspected of using drugs — because of current behavior or past history of abuse — he or she will be referred for treatment or screening.

"There are plenty of options under federal law," says Liz Schott, a welfare expert with the Center on Budget and Policy Priorities, a group that promotes government programs that support the poor. "They don't need to change their laws to do it."

Although individual drug tests run $75 or less, the costs of testing large numbers of recipients, users and non-users alike, would add up. The American Civil Liberties Union estimates that for every individual user discovered, the state's expenses would be $20,000 or more.

That runs counter to the argument proponents make that drug testing would save the state money. And it's the savings that critics say motivates bill sponsors — not the desire to help some users go straight. "The sponsor in our state said it was purely for cost savings," says Linda Katz, policy director of the Poverty Institute at Rhode Island College. "This is really just designed to demean parents on welfare."

Constitutional Questions

Katz also calls the bill "blatantly unconstitutional." A federal appellate court threw out Michigan's random drug testing law in 2003, saying it violated the constitutional ban against unreasonable search and seizure.

"Just because you're seeking public benefits doesn't mean you don't have the same kind of protection from unreasonable searches as anybody else," says Schott.

Such constitutional concerns helped shape a new law in Arizona. Welfare recipients are now asked three questions about drug use. If they answer "yes" to any, they are sent to drug testing. If they test positive, they lose benefits for a year.

Asking everyone without exception gets around some of the legal questions involved in random testing. But Schott argues it's still intrusive. Any program savings, she says, will come from people who refuse to answer such questions — preserving their constitutional rights, she says, but disqualifying themselves from receiving benefits.

Arizona believes it will save $1.7 million a year from people dropped from welfare in this way. "This isn't a benevolent statute where we want to provide services," says Ellen Katz, director of the William E. Morris Institute for Justice in Phoenix. "The whole purpose of this statute was to terminate people from the program."

Arizona's Legislature has since considered bills that would bar welfare recipients from subscribing to cable television, owning cell phones or smoking cigarettes. None of those proposals has advanced very far.

'Definitely Worth Testing'

Kelley, the Kansas legislator, thinks the constitutionality of the drug-testing regime is itself "definitely worth testing." The Michigan case was decided by a tied vote, which she believes is "hardly a definite decision against states' rights."

She says she recognizes that some people see her proposal as a "mean-spirited" attack on the poor. For that reason, she sought last month to amend her bill to apply identical drug-testing requirements to her fellow Kansas legislators.

Not surprisingly, her colleagues haven't embraced that idea. But she hasn't given up on her underlying proposal, which she describes as a "win-win" because it can help people on welfare "get out of drug dependencies, while also ensuring that tax dollars are going where they're supposed to go."

Kelley and the other state legislators promoting the drug-testing idea are tired of having their motives impugned. Blair, the West Virginia delegate, points out his state's small minority population and says his bill "is not racist at all. This bill has everything to do with helping people that are addicted to drugs get their life back."

Blair, a Republican who runs a Web site devoted to the issue called Not With My Tax Dollars, says he can't understand why the Democrats who dominate the West Virginia Legislature won't let his bill move forward. But he's not above questioning their motives as he speculates.

"The only thing I can figure out is you can't get them loaded onto the bus to go to the polls if you're taking their money from them," he says.

Welfare Alone Cannot Lift Recipients Out of Poverty

James A. Dorn

James A. Dorn is a professor of economics at Towson University and editor of the Cato Journal.

The persistence of poverty in Baltimore is disturbing. It is even more so when one looks deeper into the official data.

The 2010 American Community Survey (ACS) estimates that 25.6 percent of Baltimore's population "for whom poverty status is determined" (602,129 people) are in poverty, as measured by pre-tax income relative to the poverty threshold used by the U.S. Census Bureau. For example, if a two-person family's pre-tax money income is less than $14,218, it is considered poor; the corresponding figure for a family of four is $22,314.

However, the 25.6 percent figure doesn't tell the whole story about Baltimore's poverty.

If one looks at the ACS for families, one finds that 28 percent of Baltimore families with children under 18 are living below the poverty level. That figure rises to an astonishing 40.6 percent for female-headed families with no father present. Is it surprising that poverty persists in Baltimore?

Poverty is often blamed on high taxes, onerous regulations, barriers to occupational entry and other economic factors. But poverty is also affected by people's choices. For individuals who wait to have children, get married and stay married, obtain more education, and stay out of jail, poverty rates diminish greatly.

The poverty rate for married-couple families with related children under 18 in Baltimore is only 7.4 percent (7.5 percent for whites and 6.8 percent for blacks). Educational status is also important: Female-headed households with less than a high school degree have a poverty rate of 44.1 percent; the rate is 11 percent for those with a college degree.

With many dysfunctional families, a culture of crime, and public schools that are frequently ineffective and sometimes dangerous, the cards are stacked against poor people trying to escape poverty in Baltimore.

Government policies can influence one's choices and the level of responsibility one takes. The growth of the welfare state has eroded personal responsibility and made the poor more dependent. After spending billions on welfare programs since President Lyndon Johnson announced the War on Poverty, the U.S. poverty rate is still about the same as in 1966 (14.7 percent). How can that be?

One answer is that the official poverty statistics mismeasure the actual extent of poverty. The U.S. Census Bureau measures only pre-tax money income and ignores noncash transfer payments in the form of Medicaid (by far the largest welfare program), food stamps, children's health insurance, and child nutrition and health. If those in-kind transfers were included, the official poverty rate would decrease substantially.

Nevertheless, as Charles Murray pointed out in his landmark book "Losing Ground" (1984), even if all transfers were included as income and brought many people above the poverty thresholds, "latent poverty" would remain. That is, if welfare payments were taken away, people would return to poverty. Welfare alone cannot create wealth. Economic growth is the only sure way to reduce dependence and poverty.

Just look at China. Since 1978, when it began its march toward the market, China has achieved the world's highest sustained rate of economic growth and allowed several hundred million people to lift themselves out of absolute poverty.

Counting noncash benefits of those living in poverty in Baltimore would reduce "poverty" but not free people from welfare. A huge underclass has captured politicians for their cause of maintaining and increasing transfers rather than limiting the size and scope of government to make people more responsible and foster economic growth.

No one could say that the poor in Baltimore today are less well-off materially than 50 or 100 years ago. Indeed, if one looks at personal consumption expenditures — a better measure of one's living standard than pre-tax money income — one finds that official figures significantly overstate the extent of poverty.

Data from the U.S. Bureau of Labor Statistics show that in 2009, consumer expenditures for the lowest fifth of income earners were more than twice as high as before-tax income (which includes cash transfers and food stamps). Average annual consumption expenditures were $21,611 for the lowest quintile, while income was $9,846.

This disparity is due to underreporting of income, outside financial assistance, loans and other factors. If poverty is better measured by one's consumption rather than income, then Baltimore's 25 percent poverty rate is misleading.

Most "poor" households now have a TV, air conditioning, enough food and medical care. Many have Internet access and a cell phone (subsidized by the federal government). What they don't have is a safe environment, two parents and choice in education.

If latent poverty is to be reduced, Baltimore needs to address the problem of how to improve economic development. Part of that problem lies in heavy taxes on capital, but part also lies in the rise of government welfare and the decline in morality.

The bulk of Baltimore's budget is spent on public safety (crime reduction) and education. Government failure is evident in those areas — taxpayers are not getting their money's worth. Rather than spending more on welfare, perhaps it's time to think about how to reduce latent poverty and make people more responsible for their choices.

Poverty Has Debilitating Physical and Mental Effects

Cynthia Boyd

Cynthia Boyd, MinnPost's Community Sketchbook reporter, covers poverty, education, homelessness, mental health, aging, immigration, culture, and other topics related to the social and economic challenges facing communities.

Intriguing new research suggests a cause-and-effect relationship between poverty and poor decision-making.

And it's not the connection you may think. So-called conventional wisdom, after all, has it that making poor decisions leads to reduced living circumstances.

In contrast, the research reported in the journal Science suggests that "poverty itself" reduces cognitive capacity because "poverty-related concerns consume mental resources leaving less for other tasks."

Could it be that people of low income spend so much mental energy getting through each day balancing life's necessities against the weight of money problems that they have less capacity to deal with bigger issues that affect their lives – issues like work, education, parenting?

Yes, suggest researchers at the University of Warwick in Coventry, England.

Consequences

The consequences are significant and measurable, they say.

From the *The Guardian*:

The cognitive deficit of being preoccupied with money problems was equivalent to a loss of 13 IQ points, losing an entire night's sleep or being a chronic alcoholic, according to the study. The

"What's the relationship between poverty and poor decision-making?" by Cynthia Boyd, MinnPost, September 18, 2013. Reprinted by permission.

authors say this could explain why poorer people are more likely to make mistakes or bad decisions that exacerbate their financial difficulties.

Yet there is hope of disrupting this cycle. Continuing with *The Guardian*:

> Anandi Mani, [associate professor in economics and] a research fellow at the Centre for Competitive Advantage in the Global Economy at the University of Warwick, one of the four authors of the study, said the findings also suggest how small interventions or "nudges" at appropriate moments to help poor people access services and resources could help them break out of the poverty trap. Writing in the journal Science, Mani said that previous research has found that poor people use less preventive health care, do not stick to drug regimens, are tardier and less likely to keep appointments, are less productive workers, less attentive parents, and worse managers of their finances. "The question we therefore wanted to address is, is that a cause of poverty or a consequence of poverty?"
>
> She said the team of researchers, which included economists and psychologists in the UK and the US, wanted to test a hypothesis: "The state of worrying where your next meal is going to come from — you have uncertain income or you have more expenses than you can manage and you have to juggle all these things and constantly being pre-occupied about putting out these fires — takes up so much of your mental bandwidth, that you have less in terms of cognitive capacity to deal with things which may not be as urgent as your immediate emergency, but which are, nevertheless, important for your benefit in the medium or longer term."

The findings don't surprise Nancy A. Heitzeg, sociology professor at St. Catherine University in St. Paul.

"I think poverty does have debilitating physical and mental effects," she said, adding that she hopes the study can be used as a jumping-off point.

"Now that we have seen this research and we accept that as true, are we going to be able to turn to structural solutions for addressing this?"

In other words, she's asking is there the will in this country to change social and political policies so that the United States provides adequate services — economic, housing, food — to "minimize" poverty?

Two Sets of Studies

What researchers did was carry out two sets of studies, one at a shopping mall in New Jersey, the other among sugar-cane farmers in India.

At the mall, they approached about 400 people at random asking them to think about solving a hypothetical financial problem.

In an "easy" scenario, they needed a car repair that would cost $150, while in the "hard" scenario the repairs cost $1,500.

While thinking about the hypotheticals, the volunteers were tested with IQ-based puzzles and tasks measuring their attention.

The results, as Matt Yglesias writes for Slate, are revealing:

> Among Americans, they found that low-income people asked to ponder an expensive car repair did worse on cognitive-function tests than low-income people asked to consider cheaper repairs or than higher-income people faced with either scenario. To study the global poor, the researchers looked at performance on cognitive tests before and after the harvest among sugarcane farmers. ..... They found that the more secure postharvest farmers performed better than the more anxious preharvest ones.

The monetary affect on cognitive skills should factor in to our understanding of poverty.

Yglesias, a business and economics correspondent, sums it up this way:

Poor people — like all people — make some bad choices. There is some evidence that poor people make more of these bad choices than the average person. This evidence can easily lead to the blithe conclusion that bad choices, rather than economic conditions, are the cause of poverty. The new research shows that this is — at least to some extent — exactly backward. It's poverty itself (perhaps mediated by the unusually severe forms of decision fatigue tha[t] can affect the poor) that undermines judgment and leads to poor decision-making.

Drug-Testing Welfare Recipients Is Demeaning and a Waste of Money

Samuel Brookfield

Samuel Brookfield is an emergency registered nurse and a public health PhD candidate at the University of Queensland.

The government's announcement in the May 2017 budget of a trial of random drug testing of 5,000 Youth Allowance and Newstart recipients has been almost universally criticised. While the prime minister claimed the program is "based on love", the CEO of Jobs Australia has warned it will be so demeaning as to drive young people to sex work. And the government shows no sign of being overwhelmed by the reportedly "overwhelming" medical evidence that its policy will not work.

There is a certain amount of hyperbole on both sides of this issue, which is skewing the evidence. This makes it difficult to interpret, largely due to the lack of clarity on what the aims of this program are. Is it to help struggling addicts, reduce the number of drug users, or save money by reducing welfare payments?

Most of the evidence drawn on by critics of the trial comes from places that have implemented such programs. While it has been considered in the UK and Canada, variations on testing welfare recipients for drug use have only previously appeared in the US and New Zealand. So, have they worked? And is there a convincing link between welfare recipients and drug use at all?

Drug Use and Welfare

The most recent estimates from the US found about one in five people receiving welfare had used illicit drugs in the previous year. That makes drug use up to 50% more common in welfare households than the general population.

The impact this drug use has on their lives varies widely, however. Less than 5% of welfare recipients met the diagnostic criteria for having a substance abuse problem, which would make them eligible for withdrawal treatment.

Closer to home, a New Zealand government survey found 32% of welfare recipients reported using illicit drugs, in comparison to 18% of the general population. The clandestine nature of drug use, and the reliance on self-reporting in these statistics, make prevalence estimates imperfect. Nevertheless, drug use has been treated as a key driver of welfare dependency in the US, where testing has been implemented intermittently since the turn of the century.

Drug Testing in Florida

As numbers of such programs grew in the US, one study directly analysed the difference in employment and earnings between welfare recipients who were and were not using drugs in Florida. The study reviewed 6,642 applications as part of drug testing for the Temporary Assistance for Needy Families program. This involves the federal government providing financial assistance to pregnant women and families with one or more dependents.

The authors found a small but insignificant difference between groups, which is a difficult result on which to base conclusions. This study also didn't collect information about the extent of problematic drug use as opposed to recreational use. And it had limited ability to control for related social and demographic factors.

The confounding effect of these other factors is often alluded to as implied evidence against drug-testing programs. For instance, some studies have argued depression, physical health problems and limited education are the most common barriers to improving the conditions of drug-using welfare recipients. Yet this is not a clear argument against targeting drugs, as there is also evidence cannabis and methamphetamine use can exacerbate depression and other health conditions.

Too Costly an Exercise?

The other argument against the proposed trial, as put forward by the Australian Greens, is that it's an ineffective use of money as detection rates of drug users will be minimal. Indeed, in New Zealand, $1 million was spent on a similar scheme, which detected 22 positive results in a sample of 8,001.

Data have also been released for detection rates in a similar program in Arizona, Missouri, Utah and Tennessee over an 18-month period in 2013-14. With a total of just under 200,000 tests at a collective cost of over US$1 million, these states disqualified 14, 780, 29 and 24 people from receiving benefits, respectively.

The Australian government won't disclose the cost of its current proposal, as it is commercial in confidence. Yet A$10 million has been set aside to support welfare recipients who test positive, presumably to enter treatment or rehabilitation. In the current system, however, less than half of all people seeking drug treatment are able to get access to it. And the most recent reviews of compulsory drug treatment have reiterated it does not improve treatment outcomes.

This A$10 million alone would seem to offset any savings made from withdrawing payments following the very low numbers of positive tests that can be expected. The government has not provided any estimate of potential savings under this policy, so we don't know if this trial will save money.

What About Drug-Related Harms?

No assessment has been made thus far of how drug-related harms – such as emergency department presentations, mental health conditions, or interpersonal violence – changed in response to testing programs. But that doesn't mean we don't have reason to think such programs had no effect.

There is evidence, for example, that prohibition limits drug use. Some studies have found when addicts do enter rehabilitation, they can be motivated by the desire to avoid risk of punishment and frequent interactions with police. This would imply additional hurdles that increase the potential cost of using drugs can effectively reduce levels of use.

Some critics argue this program will penalise people with advanced levels of dependence. But to base policy on this is to ignore the evidence that addicts can and do exercise control over their drug use in response to external factors. The point at which many addicts enter treatment is usually "rock bottom", when the external motivating factors become sufficient to overpower the persistent desire to use. It's not clear how removing these factors will encourage addicts to enter treatment.

What's the Ultimate Goal?

With regards to the public health argument, the evidence exists but is unsettled and complex. This controversy is not resolved by marginalising the broader picture of relevant research. In terms of the economic argument, there is no reason to expect the costs of this program will be outweighed by the welfare payments that may be cancelled.

It can be said, as some of the architects of this program do say, that the very purpose of this trial is to collect the evidence everyone is clamouring for. The government has committed to ongoing reviews of the program and its outcomes. But this will only be useful if they answer the deeper question of what it is they're looking for.

Government Aid Programs Keep the Poor in Poverty

Charles Johnson

Charles Johnson is a Foundation for Economic Education (FEE) faculty network member as well as a writer and philosopher living and working in Auburn, Alabama.

> The experience of oppressed people is that the living of one's life is confined and shaped by forces and barriers which are not accidental or occasional and hence avoidable, but are systematically related to each other in such a way as to catch one between and among them and restrict or penalize motion in any direction. It is the experience of being caged in: all avenues, in every direction, are blocked or booby trapped.

> - Marilyn Frye, "Oppression," in The Politics of Reality

Governments—local, state, and federal—spend a lot of time wringing their hands about the plight of the urban poor. Look around any government agency and you'll never fail to find some know-it-all with a suit and a nameplate on his desk who has just the right government program to eliminate or ameliorate, or at least contain, the worst aspects of grinding poverty in American cities—especially as experienced by black people, immigrants, people with disabilities, and everyone else marked for the special observation and solicitude of the state bureaucracy. Depending on the bureaucrat's frame of mind, his pet programs might focus on doling out conditional charity to "deserving" poor people, or putting more "at-risk" poor people under the surveillance of social workers and medical experts,

"Scratching By: How Government Creates Poverty as We Know It," by Charles Johnson, FEE.org, December 1, 2007. https://fee.org/articles/scratching-by-how-government-creates-poverty-as-we-know-it/. Licensed under CC BY 4.0 International.

or beating up recalcitrant poor people and locking them in cages for several years.

But the one thing that the government and its managerial aid workers will never do is just get out of the way and let poor people do the things that poor people naturally do, and always have done, to scratch by.

Government anti-poverty programs are a classic case of the therapeutic state setting out to treat disorders created by the state itself. Urban poverty as we know it is, in fact, exclusively a creature of state intervention in consensual economic dealings. This claim may seem bold, even to most libertarians. But a lot turns on the phrase "as we know it." Even if absolute laissez faire reigned beginning tomorrow, there would still be people in big cities who are living paycheck to paycheck, heavily in debt, homeless, jobless, or otherwise at the bottom rungs of the socioeconomic ladder. These conditions may be persistent social problems, and it may be that free people in a free society will still have to come up with voluntary institutions and practices for addressing them. But in the state-regimented market that dominates today, the material predicament that poor people find themselves in—and the arrangements they must make within that predicament—are battered into their familiar shape, as if by an invisible fist, through the diffuse effects of pervasive, interlocking interventions.

Consider the commonplace phenomena of urban poverty. Livelihoods in American inner cities are typically extremely precarious: as Sudhir Alladi Venkatesh writes in *Off the Books:* "Conditions in neighborhoods of concentrated poverty can change quickly and in ways that can leave families unprepared and without much recourse." Fixed costs of living—rent, food, clothing, and so on—consume most or all of a family's income, with little or no access to credit, savings, or insurance to safeguard them from unexpected disasters.

Dependent on Others

Their poverty often leaves them dependent on other people. It pervades the lives of the employed and the unemployed alike: the jobless fall back on charity or help from family; those who live paycheck to paycheck, with little chance of finding any work elsewhere, depend on the good graces of a select few bosses and brokers. One woman quoted by Venkatesh explained why she continued to work through an exploitative labor shark rather than leaving for a steady job with a well-to-do family: "And what if that family gets rid of me? Where am I going next? See, I can't take that chance, you know. . . . All I got is Johnnie and it took me the longest just to get him on my side."

The daily experience of the urban poor is shaped by geographical concentration in socially and culturally isolated ghetto neighborhoods within the larger city, which have their own characteristic features: housing is concentrated in dilapidated apartments and housing projects, owned by a select few absentee landlords; many abandoned buildings and vacant lots are scattered through the neighborhood, which remain unused for years at a time; the use of outside spaces is affected by large numbers of unemployed or homeless people.

The favorite solutions of the welfare state—government doles and "urban renewal" projects—mark no real improvement. Rather than freeing poor people from dependence on benefactors and bosses, they merely transfer the dependence to the state, leaving the least politically connected people at the mercy of the political process.

But in a free market—a truly free market, where individual poor people are just as free as established formal-economy players to use their own property, their own labor, their own know-how, and the resources that are available to them—the informal, enterprising actions by poor people themselves would do far more to systematically undermine, or completely eliminate, each of the stereotypical conditions that welfare statists deplore. Every day and in every culture from time out of mind, poor people have repeatedly shown remarkable intelligence, courage, persistence, and creativity in finding ways to put food on the table, save money, keep safe, raise families, live full lives, learn, enjoy themselves, and experience beauty, whenever, wherever, and to whatever degree they have been free to do so. The fault for despairing, dilapidated urban ghettoes lies not in the pressures of the market, nor in the character flaws of individual poor people, nor in the characteristics of ghetto subcultures. The fault lies in the state and its persistent interference with poor people's own efforts to get by through independent work, clever hustling, scratching together resources, and voluntary mutual aid.

Housing Crisis

Progressives routinely deplore the "affordable housing crisis" in American cities. In cities such as New York and Los Angeles, about 20 to 25 percent of low-income renters are spending more than half their incomes just on housing. But it is the very laws that Progressives favor—land-use policies, zoning codes, and building codes—that ratchet up housing costs, stand in the way of alternative housing options, and confine poor people to ghetto neighborhoods. Historically, when they have been free to do so, poor people have happily disregarded the ideals of political humanitarians and found their own ways to cut housing costs, even in bustling cities with tight housing markets.

One way was to get other families, or friends, or strangers, to move in and split the rent. Depending on the number of people sharing a home, this might mean a less-comfortable living situation; it might even mean one that is unhealthy. But decisions about health and comfort are best made by the individual people who bear the costs and reap the benefits. Unfortunately today the decisions are made ahead of time by city governments through zoning laws that prohibit or restrict sharing a home among people not related by blood or marriage, and building codes that limit the number of residents in a building.

Those who cannot make enough money to cover the rent on their own, and cannot split the rent enough due to zoning and building codes, are priced out of the housing market entirely. Once homeless, they are left exposed not only to the elements, but also to harassment or arrest by the police for "loitering" or "vagrancy," even on public property, in efforts to force them into overcrowded and dangerous institutional shelters. But while government laws make living on the streets even harder than it already is, government intervention also blocks homeless people's efforts to find themselves shelter outside the conventional housing market. One of the oldest and commonest survival strategies practiced by the urban poor is to find wild or abandoned land and build shanties on it out of salvageable scrap materials. Scrap materials are plentiful, and large portions of land in ghetto neighborhoods are typically left unused as condemned buildings or vacant lots. Formal title is very often seized by the city government or by quasi-governmental "development" corporations through the use of eminent domain. Lots are held out of use, often for years at a time, while they await government public-works projects or developers willing to buy up the land for large-scale building.

Urban Homesteading

In a free market, vacant lots and abandoned buildings could eventually be homesteaded by anyone willing to do the work of occupying and using them. Poor people could use abandoned spaces within their own communities for setting up shop, for gardening, or for living space. In Miami, in October 2006, a group of community organizers and about 35 homeless people built Umoja Village, a shanty town, on an inner-city lot that the local government had kept vacant for years. They publicly stated to the local government that "We have only one demand . . . leave us alone."

That would be the end of the story in a free market: there would be no eminent domain, no government ownership, and thus also no political process of seizure and redevelopment; once-homeless people could establish property rights to abandoned land through their own sweat equity—without fear of the government's demolishing their work and selling their land out from under them. But back in Miami, the city attorney and city council took about a month to begin legal efforts to destroy the residents' homes and force them off the lot. In April 2007 the city police took advantage of an accidental fire to enforce its politically fabricated title to the land, clearing the lot, arresting 11 people, and erecting a fence to safeguard the once-again vacant lot for professional "affordable housing" developers.

Had the city government not made use of its supposed title to the abandoned land, it no doubt could have made use of state and federal building codes to ensure that residents would be forced back into homelessness—for their own safety, of course. That is in fact what a county health commission in Indiana did to a 93-year-old man named Thelmon Green, who lived in his '86 Chevrolet van, which the local towing company allowed him to keep on its lot. Many people thrown into poverty by a sudden financial catastrophe live out of a car for weeks or months until they get back on their feet. Living in a car is cramped, but it beats living on the streets: a car means a place you can have to yourself, which holds your possessions, with doors you can lock, and sometimes even air conditioning and heating. But staying in a car over the long term is much harder to manage without running afoul of the law. Thelmon Green got by well enough in his van for ten years, but when the Indianapolis Star printed a human-interest story on him last December, the county health commission took notice and promptly ordered Green evicted from his own van, in the name of the local housing code.

Since government housing codes impose detailed requirements on the size, architecture, and building materials for new permanent housing, as well as on specialized and extremely expensive contract work for electricity, plumbing, and other luxuries, they effectively obstruct or destroy most efforts to create transitional, intermediate, or informal sorts of shelter that cost less than rented space in government-approved housing projects, but provide more safety and comfort than living on the street.

Turning from expenses to income, pervasive government regulation, passed in the so-called "public interest" at the behest of comfortable middle- and upper-class Progressives, creates endless constraints on poor people's ability to earn a living or make needed money on the side.

There are, to start out, the trades that the state has made entirely illegal: selling drugs outside of a state-authorized pharmacy, prostitution outside of the occasional state-authorized brothel "ranch," or running small-time gambling operations outside of a state-authorized corporate casino. These trades are often practiced by women and men facing desperate poverty; the state's efforts add the danger of fines, forfeitures, and lost years in prison.

Poor People Shut Out

Beyond the government-created black market, there are also countless jobs that could be done above-ground, but from which the poor are systematically shut out by arbitrary regulation and licensure requirements. In principle, many women in black communities could make money braiding hair, with only their own craft, word of mouth, and the living room of an apartment. But in many states, anyone found braiding hair without having put down hundreds of dollars and days of her life to apply for a government-fabricated cosmetology or hair-care license will be fined hundreds or thousands of dollars.

In principle, anyone who knows how to cook can make money by laying out the cash for ingredients and some insulated containers, and taking the food from his own kitchen to a stand set up on the sidewalk or, with the landlord's permission, in a parking lot. But then there are business licenses to pay for (often hundreds of dollars) and the costs of complying with health-department regulations and inspections. The latter make it practically impossible to run a food-oriented business without buying or leasing property dedicated to preparing the food, at which point you may as well forget about it unless you already have a lot of start-up capital sitting around.

Every modern urban center has a tremendous demand for taxi cabs. In principle, anyone who needed to make some extra money could start a part-time "gypsy cab" service with a car she already has, a cell phone, and some word of mouth. She can make good money for honest labor, providing a useful service to willing customers—as a single independent worker, without needing to please a boss, who can set her own hours and put as much or as little into it as she wants in order to make the money she needs.

But in the United States, city governments routinely impose massive constraints and controls on taxi service. The worst offenders are often the cities with the highest demand for cabs, like New York City, where the government enforces an arbitrary cap on the number of taxi cabs through a system of government-created licenses, or "medallions." The total number of medallion taxis is capped at about 13,000 cabs for the entire city, with occasional government auctions for a handful of new medallions. The system requires anyone who wants to become an independent cab driver to purchase a medallion at monopoly prices from an existing holder or wait around for the city to auction off new ones. At the auction last November a total of 63 new medallions were made available for auction with a minimum bidding price of $189,000.

Besides the cost of a medallion, cab owners are also legally required to pay an annual licensing fee of $550 and to pay for three inspections by the city government each year, at a total annual cost of $150. The city government enforces a single fare structure, enforces a common paint job, and now is even forcing all city cabs to upgrade to high-cost, high-tech GPS and payment systems, whether or not the cabbie or her customer happens to want them. The primary beneficiary of this politically imposed squeeze on independent cabbies is VeriFone Holdings, the first firm approved to sell the electronic systems to a captive market. Doug Bergeron, VeriFone's CEO, crows that "Every year, we find a free ride on a new segment of the economy that is going electronic." In this case, VeriFone is enjoying a "free ride" indeed.

The practical consequence is that poor people who might otherwise be able to make easy money on their own are legally forced out of driving a taxi, or else forced to hire themselves out to an existing medallion-holder on his own terms. Either way, poor people are shoved out of flexible, independent work, which many would be willing and able to do using one of the few capital goods that they already have on hand. Lots of poor people have cars they could use; not a lot have a couple hundred thousand dollars to spend on a government-created license.

Government regimentation of land, housing, and labor creates and sustains the very structure of urban poverty. Government seizures create and reinforce the dilapidation of ghetto neighborhoods by constricting the housing market to a few landlords and keeping marginal lands out of use. Government regulations create homelessness and artificially make it worse for the homeless by driving up housing costs and by obstructing or destroying any intermediate informal living solutions between renting an apartment and living on the street. And having made the ghetto, government prohibitions keep poor people confined in it, by shutting them out of more affluent neighborhoods where many might be able to live if only they were able to share expenses.

Ratcheting Costs Up and Opportunities Down

Artificially limiting the alternative options for housing ratchets up the fixed costs of living for the urban poor. Artificially limiting the alternative options for independent work ratchets down the opportunities for increasing income. And the squeeze makes poor people dependent on—and thus vulnerable to negligent or unscrupulous treatment from—both landlords and bosses by constraining their ability to find other, better homes, or other, better livelihoods. The same squeeze puts many more poor people into the position of living "one paycheck away" from homelessness and makes that position all the more precarious by harassing and coercing and imposing artificial destitution on those who do end up on the street.

American state corporatism forcibly reshapes the world of work and business on the model of a commercial strip mall: sanitized, centralized, regimented, officious, and dominated by a few powerful proprietors and their short list of favored partners, to whom everyone else relates as either an employee or a consumer. A truly free market, without the pervasive control of state licensure requirements, regulation, inspections, paperwork, taxes, "fees," and the rest, has much more to do with the traditional image of a bazaar: messy, decentralized, diverse, informal, flexible, pervaded by haggling, and kept together by the spontaneous order of countless small-time independent operators, who quickly and easily shift between the roles of customer, merchant, contract laborer, and more. It is precisely because we have the strip mall rather than the bazaar that people living in poverty find themselves so often confined to ghettoes, caught in precarious situations, and dependent on others—either on the bum or caught in jobs they hate but cannot leave, while barely keeping a barely tolerable roof over their heads.

The poorer you are, the more you need access to informal and flexible alternatives, and the more you need opportunities to apply some creative hustling. When the state shuts that out, it shuts poor people into ghettoized poverty.

CHAPTER 4

Will Overcoming Learned Helplessness End the Culture of Poverty?

The Cycle of Poverty Can Lead to Learned Helplessness

Kendra Cherry

Kendra Cherry is an author and educator with over a decade of experience helping students make sense of psychology.

When bad things happen, we like to believe that we would do whatever necessary to change the situation. Research on what is known as learned helplessness has shown that when people feel like they have no control over what happens, they tend to simply give up and accept their fate.

What Is Learned Helplessness?

Learned helplessness occurs when an animal is repeatedly subjected to an aversive stimulus that it cannot escape.

Eventually, the animal will stop trying to avoid the stimulus and behave as if it is utterly helpless to change the situation. Even when opportunities to escape are presented, this learned helplessness will prevent any action.

While the concept is strongly tied to animal psychology and behavior, it can also apply to many situations involving human beings.

When people feel that they have no control over their situation, they may also begin to behave in a helpless manner. This inaction can lead people to overlook opportunities for relief or change.

The Discovery of Learned Helplessness

The concept of learned helplessness was discovered accidentally by psychologists Martin Seligman and Steven F. Maier. They had initially observed helpless behavior in dogs that were classically conditioned to expect an electrical shock after hearing a tone.

"What Is Learned Helplessness and Why Does it Happen?" by Kendra Cherry, Verywell Mind, June 24, 2017. Reprinted by permission.

Later, the dogs were placed in a shuttlebox that contained two chambers separated by a low barrier.

The floor was electrified on one side, and not on the other. The dogs previously subjected to the classical conditioning made no attempts to escape, even though avoiding the shock simply involved jumping over a small barrier.

To investigate this phenomenon, the researchers then devised another experiment.

- In group one, the dogs were strapped into harnesses for a period of time and then released.
- The dogs in the second group were placed in the same harnesses but were subjected to electrical shocks that could be avoided by pressing a panel with their noses.
- The third group received the same shocks as those in group two, except that those in this group were not able to control the shock. For those dogs in the third group, the shocks seemed to be completely random and outside of their control.

The dogs were then placed in a shuttlebox. Dogs from the first and second group quickly learned that jumping the barrier eliminated the shock. Those from the third group, however, made no attempts to get away from the shocks. Due to their previous experience, they had developed a cognitive expectation that nothing they did would prevent or eliminate the shocks.

Learned Helplessness in People

The impact of learned helplessness has been demonstrated in different animal species, but its effects can also be seen in people.

Consider one often-used example: A child who performs poorly on math tests and assignments will quickly begin to feel that *nothing* he does will have any effect on his math performance. When later faced with any type of math-related task, he may experience a sense of helplessness.

Learned helplessness has also been associated with several different psychological disorders. Depression, anxiety, phobias, shyness, and loneliness can all be exacerbated by learned helplessness.

For example, a woman who feels shy in social situations may eventually begin to feel that there is nothing she can do to overcome her symptoms. This sense that her symptoms are out of her direct control may lead her to stop trying to engage herself in social situations, thus making her shyness even more pronounced.

Researchers have found, however, that learned helplessness does not always generalize across all settings and situations.

A student who experiences learned helpless with regards to math class will not necessarily experience that same helplessness when faced with performing calculations in the real-world. In other cases, people may experience learned helplessness that generalizes across a wide variety of situations.

So what explains why some people develop learned helplessness and others do not? Why is it specific to some situations but more global in others?

Many researchers believe that attribution or explanatory styles play a role in determining how people are impacted by learned helplessness. This view suggests that an individual's characteristic style of explaining events helps determine whether or not they will develop learned helplessness. A pessimistic explanatory style is associated with a greater likelihood of experiencing learned helplessness. People with this explanatory style tend to view negative as being inescapable and unavoidable and tend to take personal responsibility for such negative events.

So what can people do to overcome learned helplessness? Cognitive-behavioral therapy is form of psychotherapy that can be beneficial in overcoming the thinking and behavioral patterns that contribute to learned helplessness.

A Word from Verywell

Learned helplessness can have a profound impact on mental health and well-being. People who experience learned helplessness are also likely to experience symptoms of depression, elevated stress levels, and less motivation to take care of their physical health.

If you feel that learned helplessness might be having a negative impact on your life and health, consider talking to your doctor about steps you can take to address this type of thinking.

Having the Right Mindset Can Lift an American Out of Poverty

Pam Fessler

Pam Fessler is a correspondent on NPR's national desk, where she covers poverty and philanthropy. Through her journalistic work on poverty she received the 2011 First Place Headliner award in the human interest category.

When it comes to poor Americans, the Trump administration has a message: Government aid is holding many of them back. Without it, many more of them would be working.

Office of Management and Budget (OMB) Director Mick Mulvaney said as much when presenting the administration's budget plan this week to cut safety net programs by hundreds of billions of dollars over the next 10 years. The administration also wants to tighten work requirements for those getting aid, such as food stamps, or Supplemental Nutrition Assistance Program (SNAP) benefits.

"If you're on food stamps, and you're able-bodied, we need you to go to work. If you're on disability insurance and you're not supposed to be — if you're not truly disabled, we need you to go back to work," he said.

On Wednesday night, Housing and Urban Development Secretary Ben Carson — whose budget to help low-income households would be cut by more than $6 billion next year — added his own thoughts. He said in a radio interview that "poverty to a large extent is also a state of mind."

Carson — who himself grew up in poverty to become a widely acclaimed neurosurgeon — said people with the "right mind set" can have everything taken away from them, and they'll pull themselves up. He believes the converse is true as well. "You take somebody with the wrong mind-set, you can give them everything in the world (and) they'll work their way right back down to the bottom," Carson said.

Anti-poverty advocates say both Carson and Mulvaney are fundamentally wrong, that most low-income people would work if they could. And many of them already do. They just don't make enough to live on.

"All Americans, but particularly one of the top federal anti-poverty officials, should understand that the main causes of U.S. poverty are economic, not mental," said Joel Berg, CEO of Hunger Free America. "Overwhelming facts and data prove that the main causes of poverty are low wages, too few jobs, and an inadequate safety net – not some sort of personal attitude problem."

He and other advocates say the image of millions of able-bodied people sitting around collecting checks doesn't match reality. About two-thirds of the 42 million people who get SNAP benefits are elderly, disabled or children. A majority of SNAP families with kids have at least one person who's working, according to the U.S. Department of Agriculture.

Olivia Golden, executive director of the nonpartisan Center for Law and Social Policy (CLASP), says one of the biggest obstacles to getting people off government aid is the lack of decent-paying jobs.

"Two-thirds of poor children live with an adult who's working," she says. "So working is no guarantee of being above poverty."

Golden says Carson's suggestion that poor people are lazy or somehow at fault is "an idea that through American history has been an excuse for really bad policy decisions." She cited lack of investments in education, and says the comments are especially egregious given the president's budget proposal. It calls for steep cuts in education, health care, job training and other supports for low-income Americans.

Golden argues that, rather than discourage work, government support — such a food aid and health care — can encourage people to seek and keep jobs by helping them to stabilize their lives. She says it's easier to work if you aren't worried about being hungry or sick.

Michael Tanner of the libertarian Cato Institute also thinks Carson is wrong about poverty being a state of mind. "Poverty is being poor," says Tanner.

But he agrees that government benefits can sometimes be a disincentive to working, because people make an economic decision about whether they'll be better off if they take a job. By the time they calculate the loss of benefits, taxes they'll have to pay and the cost of employment — such as child care and transportation — it's often not worth it.

He also thinks that some people stuck in poverty do make bad choices — such as dropping out of school or getting pregnant — that worsen their economic outlook.

But Tanner says many poor Americans have to deal with conditions that are not of their making and prevent them from getting ahead. He thinks the answer isn't cutting government aid, but dealing with the barriers to work, including a lack of education and a criminal justice system that leaves many — especially African-American men — with criminal records that prevent them from getting hired.

Joel Berg thinks raising the minimum wage would also help, as would making housing more affordable for low-income families. The Trump budget would cut some of these programs, overseen by HUD Secretary Carson.

In presenting the budget, OMB Director Mulvaney did offer this assurance for those people who are getting government aid. "We are going to do everything we can to help you find a job that you are suited to and a job that you can use to help take care of you, yourself, and your family," he said.

He didn't provide details other than to add, "If you're in this country and you want to work, there's good news, because Donald Trump is President and we're going to get 3 percent growth, and we're going to give you the opportunity to go back to work."

Mulvaney also promised that the administration would not kick "anybody off of any program who really needs it ... we have plenty of money in this country to take care of the people who need it."

Defining just who does and doesn't "need it" will likely be a big part of the debate as Congress considers what to do with the president's plans.

Poverty Affects Classroom Engagement

Eric Jensen

Eric Jensen is a San Diego-based educator and author. He holds an MA in organizational development and a PhD in human development. He is known for his translation of neuroscience into practical classroom applications.

Poverty is an uncomfortable word. I'm often asked, "What should I expect from kids from low-income households?" Typically, teachers are unsure what to do differently.

Just as the phrase *middle class* tells us little about a person, the word *poverty* typically tells us little about the students we serve. We know, for example, that the poor and middle classes have many overlapping values, including valuing education and the importance of hard work (Gorski, 2008). But if poor people were exactly the same cognitively, socially, emotionally, and behaviorally as those from the middle class, then the exact same teaching provided to both middle-class students and students from poverty would bring the exact same results.

But it doesn't work that way. In one study of 81,000 students across the United States, the students not in Title I programs consistently reported higher levels of engagement than students who were eligible for free or reduced-price lunch (Yazzie-Mintz, 2007). Are children from poverty more likely to struggle with engagement in school?

The answer is yes.

[…]

Effort

Uninformed teachers may think that poor children slouch, slump, and show little effort because they are—or their parents are—lazy.

"How Poverty Affects Classroom Engagement," by Eric Jensen, Association for Supervision and Curriculum Development (ASCD), May 2013. Reprinted by permission.

Yet research suggests that parents from poor families work as much as parents of middle- or upper-class families do (Economic Policy Institute, 2002). There's no "inherited laziness" passed down from parents.

One reason many students seem unmotivated is because of lack of hope and optimism. Low socioeconomic status and the accompanying financial hardships are correlated with depressive symptoms (Butterworth, Olesen, & Leach, 2012). Moreover, the passive "I give up" posture may actually be learned helplessness, shown for decades in the research as a symptom of a stress disorder and depression. Research from 60 high-poverty schools tells us that the primary factor in student motivation and achievement isn't the student's home environment; it's the school and the teacher (Irvin, Meece, Byun, Farmer, & Hutchins, 2011). Effort can be taught, and strong teachers do this every day.

Students who show little or no effort are simply giving you feedback. When you liked your teacher, you worked harder. When the learning got you excited, curious, and intrigued, you put out more effort. We've all seen how students will often work much harder in one class than in another. The feedback is about themselves—and about your class.

Take on the challenge. Invest in students who are not putting out effort. In a study of more than 1,800 children from poverty, school engagement was a key factor in whether the student stayed in school (Finn & Rock, 1997).

What You Can Do

First, strengthen your relationships with students by revealing more of yourself and learning more about your students. Ask yourself, "What have I done to build relationships and respect? Do my students like me?"

Use more buy-in strategies, such as curiosity builders (a mystery box or bag); excitement and risk ("This idea's a bit crazy; let's make sure we have the number for the fire department, just in case"); and competition ("My last class accomplished _____;

let's see what you can do!"). Make the learning more of the students' idea by offering a choice, and involve them more in decision making.

Second, teachers must make connections to students' worlds in ways that help them see a viable reason to play the academic game. Can you tie classroom learning to the real world? Use money, shopping, technology, and their family members to make the learning more relevant. Without clear links between the two, students often experience a demotivating disconnect between the school world and their home life. As a result, they give up.

Third, affirm effort every day in class. Most teachers don't keep track of their comments to students; maybe they should. When teachers give more positives than negatives (a 3:1 ratio is best), they optimize both learning and growth (Fredrickson & Losada, 2005). When affirmed, challenged, and encouraged, students work harder.

Fourth, set high goals and sell students on their chances to reach them. Get them to believe in the goals by showing them real-world success stories of adults who came from the same circumstances the students did and who achieved their goals.

Finally, provide daily feedback so students see that effort matters and that they can adjust it for even greater success. Affirm your students, and let them know how much good you see in them.

Hope and the Growth Mind-Set

Hope is a powerful thing. Research suggests that lower socioeconomic status is often associated with viewing the future as containing more negative events than positive ones (Robb, Simon, & Wardle, 2009). Low or no expectancy ("helplessness") is also related to low socioeconomic status (Odéen et al., 2012). In short, being poor is associated with lowered expectations about future outcomes.

The student's attitude about learning (his or her mind-set) is also a moderately robust predictive factor (Blackwell, Trzesniewski, & Dweck, 2007). Taken together, hope—or the lack of hope—and mind-set—whether you believe that you're simply born smart or that you can grow in intelligence along the way—can be either significant assets or serious liabilities. If students think failure or low performance is likely, they'll probably not bother to try. Similarly, if they think they aren't smart enough and can't succeed, they'll probably not put out any effort.

What You Can Do

Teacher and student beliefs about having a fixed amount of "smarts" that the student can't increase will influence engagement and learning. Teach students that their brains can change and grow, that they can even raise their IQs. Provide better-quality feedback (prompt, actionable, and task-specific).

Also, telling students that they have a limited amount of focusing power is likely to disengage many of them (Miller et al., 2012). There's an alternative to saying, "Don't feel bad that you didn't finish. It's late in the day, and we've all got brain drain." Instead, say, "Stick with this just a bit longer. You can do this! Your mind is a powerful force to help you reach your goals."

Don't use comforting phrases that imply that even though a student isn't good at something, he or she has "other" strengths (Cooper, 2012). Instead, focus on affirming and reinforcing effort. Guide students in making smarter strategy choices and cultivating a positive attitude.

Cognition

Children from lower socioeconomic backgrounds often perform below those from higher socioeconomic backgrounds on tests of intelligence and academic achievement (Bradley & Corwyn, 2002). Commonly, low-SES children show cognitive problems, including short attention spans, high levels of distractibility, difficulty monitoring the quality of their work, and difficulty generating new solutions to problems (Alloway, Gathercole, Kirkwood, & Elliott, 2009). These issues can make school harder for children from impoverished backgrounds.

Many children who struggle cognitively either act out (exhibit problem behavior) or shut down (show learned helplessness).

But cognitive capacity, as well as intelligence, is a teachable skill (Buschkuehl & Jaeggi, 2010).

If you're not teaching core cognitive skills, rethink your teaching methods. Students who struggle with reading, math, and following directions may have weak vocabulary, poor working memory, or poor processing skills. Studies show that high-performing teachers can overcome the problems of underperforming kids (Ferguson, 1998). Like effort, cognitive capacity is teachable.

What You Can Do

Focus on the core academic skills that students need the most. Begin with the basics, such as how to organize, study, take notes, prioritize, and remember key ideas. Then teach problem-solving, processing, and working-memory skills.

Start small. Teach students immediate recall of words, then phrases, then whole sentences. This will help them remember the directions you give in class and will support them as they learn how to do mental computations. This will take tons of encouragement, positive feedback, and persistence. Later, you can use this foundation to build higher-level skills.

Relationships

When children's early experiences are chaotic and one or both of the parents are absent, the developing brain often becomes insecure and stressed. Three-quarters of all children from poverty have a single-parent caregiver.

In homes of those from poverty, children commonly get twice as many reprimands as positive comments, compared with a 3:1 ratio of positives to negatives in middle-class homes (Risley & Hart, 2006). If caregivers are stressed about health care, housing, and food, they're more likely to be grumpy and less likely to offer positive comments to their kids.

The probability of dropping out and school failure increases as a function of the timing and length of time that children are exposed to relational adversity (Spilt, Hughes, Wu, & Kwok,

2012). Having only a single caregiver in the home—if the father is absent, for example—can create both instability and uncertainty because the children are missing a role model. Two caregivers offer the luxury of a backup—when one parent is at work, busy, or overly stressed, the other can provide for the children so there's always a stabilizing force present. Relationships can be challenging for children who lack role models and sufficient supports.

Low-income parents are often less able than middle-class parents to adjust their parenting to the demands of their higher-needs children (Paulussen-Hoogeboom, Stams, Hermanns, & Peetsma, 2007). For example, many parents don't know what to do with children who have attention deficit hyperactivity disorder (ADHD), who are oppositional, or who are dyslexic.

Disruptive home relationships often create mistrust in students. Adults have often failed them at home, and children may assume that the adults in school will fail them, too. Classroom misbehaviors are likely because many children simply do not have the at-home stability or repertoire of necessary social-emotional responses for school. Students are more likely to be impulsive, use inappropriate language, and act disrespectful—until you teach them more appropriate social and emotional responses.

What You Can Do

Children with unstable home lives are particularly in need of strong, positive, caring adults. The more you care, the better the foundation for interventions. Learn every student's name. Ask about their family, their hobbies, and what's important to them. Stop telling students what to do and start teaching them how to do it.

For example, if you ask a high school student to dial down his or her energy for the next few minutes and the student responds with a smirk or wisecrack, simply ask him or her to stay a moment after class. Never embarrass the student in front of his or her peers. After class, first reaffirm your relationship with the student. Then demonstrate the behavior you wanted (show the student the appropriate facial expression and posture); say why it will be important as the student moves through school ("This will keep you out of trouble with other adults"); and indicate when a given response is appropriate and what it should look like ("When you think your teacher has overstepped his or her bounds, this is what you should say"). End by affirming common goals and interests ("We're both in this together. We can make this work—if we each do our part").

Distress

Although small amounts of stress are healthy, acute and chronic stress—known as distress—is toxic. Children living in poverty experience greater chronic stress than do their more affluent counterparts. Low-income parents' chronic stress affects their kids through chronic activation of their children's immune systems, which taxes available resources and has long-reaching effects (Blair & Raver, 2012). Distress affects brain development, academic success, and social competence (Evans, Kim, Ting, Tesher, & Shannis, 2007). It also impairs behaviors; reduces attentional control (Liston, McEwen, & Casey, 2009); boosts impulsivity (Evans, 2003); and impairs working memory (Evans & Schamberg, 2009).

Distressed children typically exhibit one of two behaviors: angry "in your face" assertiveness or disconnected "leave me alone" passivity. To the uninformed, the student may appear to be either out of control, showing an attitude, or lazy. But those behaviors are actually symptoms of stress disorders—and distress influences many behaviors that influence engagement.

The more aggressive behaviors include talking back to the teacher, getting in the teacher's face, using inappropriate body language, and making inappropriate facial expressions. The more passive behaviors include failing to respond to questions or requests, exhibiting passivity, slumping or slouching, and disconnecting from peers or academic work.

What You Can Do

Address the real issue—distress—and the symptoms will diminish over time. Begin by building stronger relationships with students; this helps alleviate student stress.

Reduce stress by embedding more classroom fun in academics. Provide temporary cognitive support—that is, help students get the extra glucose and oxygen they need—by having them engage in such sensory motor activities as the childhood game "head-toes-knees-shoulders," in which children touch different parts of their bodies in quick succession. Such actions can support behavioral regulation, which is so important for early academic success.

Next, don't try to exert more control over the student's life. This will only create continued issues with engagement. Instead, give students more control over their own daily lives at school. Encourage responsibility and leadership by offering choices, having students engage in projects, and supporting teamwork and classroom decision making. Having a sense of control is the fundamental element that helps diminish the effects of chronic and acute stress.

Finally, teach students ongoing coping skills so they can better deal with their stressors. For example, give them a simple, "If this, then that" strategy for solving problems using new skills. You can do this through telling stories about your own daily stressors, allowing students to brainstorm solutions, and then sharing the coping tools that worked for you and modeling how you addressed various challenges.

Seeing Clearly

Remember, students in poverty are not broken or damaged. In fact, human brains adapt to experiences by making changes—and your students can change.

You can help them do so by understanding these seven differences and addressing these differences with purposeful teaching. Your school can join the ranks of the many high-performing Title I schools where students succeed every day.

The Science of Learned Helplessness

Scott Santens

Scott Santens is a writer based in New Orleans who focuses on humanity's potential for improvement.

At the end of 2015, after a year-long journey, I achieved the realization of an idea with the help of about 140 people that has already forever changed the way I look at the very foundations—*or lack thereof*—upon which all of society is based. I now firmly believe we have the potential through its universal adoption to systemically transform society for the better, even more so than many of those most familiar with the idea have long postulated, because for me, the idea is no longer just an idea. It's not theory. It is part of my life. It's real. And the effects are undeniable for someone actually living with it.

The idea of which I speak goes by the name of "basic income" but is best understood not by name, but by function, and that function is simply to provide a monthly universal starting point located above the poverty line as a new secure foundation for existence. It's an irrevocable stipend for life. In the U.S. it would be something like $1,000 for every citizen every month. All other income would then be earned as additional income on top of it so that employment would always pay more than unemployment.

This may sound overly expensive, but it would save far more than it costs. It would also really only require an additional net transfer of around $900 billion, and that's without subtracting the existing welfare programs it could replace, and also without simplifying the tax code through the replacement of all the many credits, deductions, and subsidies it could also replace. Basically we're already handing out money to everyone, rich and poor alike, but in hundreds of different ways through thousands of government middlemen who only serve to disincentivize employment by removing government supports as a reward for working.

Odds are this idea is new to you, but it's not a new idea. It's been considered for hundreds of years from as long ago in the U.S. by founding father Thomas Paine in the 18th century, to Richard Nixon, Martin Luther King, Jr., and free market-loving Milton Friedman in the 20th century, to a quickly growing list of new names here in the 21st century. Its advocates know no ideological lines. Supporters include Nobel prize-winning economists, libertarians, progressives, conservatives, climate change activists, tax reformers, feminists, anarchists, doctors, human rights defenders, racial justice leaders, and the list goes on.

For such an old idea that's been endorsed by so many for so long and yet has obviously never yet come to be, you may be thinking, "Why now?" The answer to such a question has economic reasoning rooted in the globalization of labor and the exponential advancement of technologies capable of entirely replacing labor, but as important as this particular discussion is to have, it's centered more around the idea of a future problem and less a present one.

However, our problems are very much in the present and to see why, we need to go deeper, much deeper, beyond technology and economics, and into human biology itself. To do that, we'll first need to look at what we as humans have learned from some animals in the lab and in the wild, because I think doing so pulls back the curtain on our entire social system.

Animals in Cages

As is true with many scientific discoveries, they tend to be accidental, and the story of Martin Seligman and some dogs back in 1965 is no different. Seligman wanted to know if dogs could be classically conditioned to react to bells in the same way as if they'd just been shocked, so he put them in a crate with a floor that could be electrified, and shocked them each time he rang a bell. The dogs soon began to react to the bell as if they'd just been shocked. Next however, he put them in a special crate where they could leap to safety to avoid the shock, and this is where the surprise happened.

The dogs wouldn't leap to safety. It turns out they'd learned from the prior part of the experiment that it didn't matter what they did. The shock would come anyway. They had learned helplessness. Seligman then tried the experiment with dogs who had not been shocked and they leaped to safety just as expected. But the dogs who had learned helplessness, they just sadly laid down and whimpered.

Fast forward to 1971 where a scientist named Jay Weiss explored this further with rats in cages. He put three rats into three different cages with electrodes attached to their tails and a wheel for each to turn. One rat was the lucky rat. No shocks were involved. Another would get shocks that could be stopped by turning its wheel. The third was the unlucky one. It would get shocked at the same time as the second rat, but it could do nothing about it. The third rat would only stop getting shocked when the second rat turned its wheel. Can you guess what happened?

Even though the two rats that were shocked got shocked at the same time and for the same duration of time, their outcomes were very different. The rat who had the power to stop the pain was just a bit worse off than the rat who experienced no pain at all. However, the rat who had no control whatsoever, stuck with a lever that did nothing, became heavily ulcerated. Like the dog, it too had learned helplessness. The cost of this lesson was its health.

The Power of Perception

Of course humans are not dogs or rats. There's a bit more complexity when it comes to us and our physiological responses. For us, perception is a key factor. This is where something called attribution comes into play, of which there are three important kinds that lead to humans learning helplessness: internal, stable, and global.

Think back to when you first started school and try to remember your first math test. What if after taking that first test you did poorly on it, and instead of all the other possible reasons for why that could happen, you decided it was because you sucked at math? That's an internal attribution. Now imagine you applied that attribution to all math tests. That's a stable attribution. It's not a one time thing. Now imagine you applied it beyond math to all classes. That's a global attribution. Consider the results of such perceptions.

Maybe that first math test was simply too hard for everyone in the class. Maybe it wasn't just you. Maybe your poor grade was due to not studying hard enough, or because you were too hungry or too tired. But instead, because you decided it was your fault and it meant you were stupid, your entire life went down a different path. Even though at any point along the way, you could have escaped that path, just like Seligman's dogs could have escaped the shocks, what if you had learned helplessness from that first math test?

It's even been shown that we only need to be *told* there's nothing we can do in order for us to feel there's no point in trying. It's like a self-fulfilling prophecy. Tell everyone there's no point in voting, and fewer people will vote.

What all of this shows is two-fold and extremely important to remember. We can learn to be helpless in an environment that actually offers us control, and the *feeling* itself of control can be the difference between a life full of unending stress, and a relatively stress-free life.

Fight or Flight

Stress is more than a feeling. Stress is a physiological response, and it has important evolutionary reasons for being. Back in the day, many thousands of years ago, our ancestors who could shift into a kind of emergency gear where long-term higher-order creative thinking shut down, and the body was enabled to think faster, react quicker, be stronger, move faster, run longer, and think only about survival… those were the humans who survived.

We call this now the fight-or-flight response, and where this once incredibly important response was evolutionarily adaptive, it is now maladaptive. We don't live in that same world anymore where it made so much sense. We aren't being chased down by lions or being eaten by wolves while sitting in front of our computers in our air-conditioned offices, and yet our fight-or-flight responses are still being activated. In fact, for far too many, daily existence is nothing but fight-or-flight. Long-term stress is a real problem, and I would argue, it's not just a health problem. It's a problem for human civilization.

Sapolsky and Stress

One of the most knowledgeable scientists in the world in this area is Robert Sapolsky, a pioneering neuroendocrinologist and professor at Stanford University who has spent more than thirty years studying the effects of stress on health, of which there are many. Over the years, Sapolsky has found that long-term stress increases one's risk of diabetes, cardiac problems, and gastrointestinal disorders. Stress suppresses the immune system. It causes reproductive dysfunction in men and women. It suppresses growth in kids. It affects developing fetuses. Newer evidence even shows it causes faster aging of DNA. But potentially worst of all is what it does to the human mind.

Prolonging fight-or-flight into a chronic condition means that neurons in the brain related to things like learning, memory, and judgment all suffer the consequences thanks to the wide-ranging effects of our double-edged sword stress hormones called glucocorticoids. Recent research has even shown this response made chronic is a self-perpetuating cycle. A constantly stressed out brain appears to lead to a kind of hardening of neural pathways. Essentially, feeling chronic stress makes it harder to not perceive stress, creating a vicious cycle of unending stress.

On top of this, and related back to Weiss's rats and human attribution theory, is the coping responses of those who are stressed out. Think of the "off-lever" in the second rat's cage. There are many such levers around us and although they can be effective in reducing our stress levels, many of them are arguably pretty bad off-switches. These responses include acting out against others, otherwise known as displacement aggression or bullying.

Yes, bullying is an effective coping mechanism. As the saying goes, sh*t rolls downhill, and there's actually a scientific reason for that other than gravity. In a hierarchy, it is healthier after a loss to start another fight with someone you can beat, than to mope about the loss. The former is the abdication of control, a form of learned helplessness, and the latter is the creation of control, a kind of learned aggressiveness.

Life in the 21st century is full of both. On the learned helplessness side, there have been an estimated 45,000 suicides per year since 2000, with a sharp rise since 2007, that can all be attributed to the stresses surrounding the economic insecurities of unemployment and underemployment. The U.S. is even confounding the world, with a mysterious and dramatic rise in mortality rates among middle-aged white men and women, who all appear to be drinking and overdosing themselves to death.

On the displacement aggression side, we see bullying of traditionally marginalized groups and a global and marked increase of anti-immigrant sentiment which has already led directly to the election of Donald Trump and as a result, cries for border walls and travel bans. We are seeing a rise in authoritarianism, which is fundamentally a cry for more control and predictability.

A society full of unhealthy people getting sick more than they otherwise would be, saddled with difficulties learning and remembering, suffering from weakened judgment and short-term survival thinking, and violently turning on each other as a means of coping is not a recipe for success. It's a recipe for disaster, especially faced with species-endangering challenges like climate change that demand long-term thinking. But there is hope, and that hope springs from the same well as our problems.

[...]

Stressed Out Humans

All of this goes a long way toward explaining a great deal of human behavior. The construction of a social hierarchy is a naturally emergent phenomenon of our biology. Being "above" someone else in rank offers a level of control and predictability. Our personalities help determine our ranks and also how we cope with a lack of control and predictability. Our social relationships help put our lives and the world around us into perspective. However, this is no meritocracy and much depends on the circumstances of birth.

Growing Immobility

Because our personalities are greatly determined by our environments, especially as kids, a positive feedback loop can emerge where those born and raised in high stress environments full of impoverishment and inequality are unable to escape those environments. This can then become self-perpetuating through each successive generation that follows. We see this happening right now. For all those born into the bottom fifth of American society, about half remain there as adults. The same is true for the top fifth. Meanwhile, the middle 60% are twice as mobile as either one. If we care about the American Dream, we should consider the implications.

Growing Violence

What's the result of such generational stratification of little social mobility? One need look no further than our coping mechanisms—the levers of control we create—to understand why so many things we don't want, emerge from highly unequal societies. Remember displacement aggression? A 1990 study of 50 countries concluded economic inequality is so significantly related to rates of homicide despite an extensive list of conceptually relevant controls, that a decrease in income inequality of 0.01 Gini (a measure of inequality) leads to 12.7 fewer homicides per 100,000 individuals. Simply put, and this is a robust finding, growing inequality leads to growing violence. A meta-analysis of 34 separate studies even found 97% of the correlations reported between social inequality and violent crime to be positive, meaning as one got bigger or smaller, the other got bigger or smaller.

Growing Addictions

Addictions are another result. Drug use is a lever of control that is also an escape. We may not be able to control anything around us, but we can control an entirely personal decision that is as simple as drinking that vodka or smoking that cigarette. It can function as the middle finger to everything and everyone around us as a way of saying, "I may be stuck in this cage, but you can't stop me from using this to feel like I've escaped, if only temporarily, and if even only an illusion. This is me controlling the one thing I can control—myself." Consider again the mysteriously growing mortality rates of middle-aged white people due to overdoses and liver disease.

As economic inequality increases, other scientifically correlated effects include: reduced trust and civic engagement, eroded social cohesion, higher infant mortality rates, lower overall life expectancy, more mental illness, reduced educational outcomes, higher rates of imprisonment, increased teen pregnancy rates, greater rates of obesity, and the list continues to grow as inequality-related research grows.

Additionally, if you look closely at such a list of effects, it shows the erosion of social supports. If you are less likely to trust your neighbor, if you aren't as involved in your community, if you or those you interact with are more aggressive, if you are depressed and just want to be alone, that means the all important trump card for handling stress—social connectedness—vanishes. This too is its own feedback loop. Less social connection means more stress which means less social connection. It's an unending cycle for human misery.

It's also exactly what we've been observing in the United States for decades. Robert Putnam wrote an entire book about it back in

2000 titled "Bowling Alone." The title originated from the statistic that although more people are bowling, less people are doing it in leagues. As observed by Putnam:

> *"Community and equality are mutually reinforcing... Social capital and economic inequality moved in tandem through most of the twentieth century. In terms of the distribution of wealth and income, America in the 1950s and 1960s was more egalitarian than it had been in more than a century... Those same decades were also the high point of social connectedness and civic engagement. Record highs in equality and social capital coincided. Conversely, the last third of the twentieth century was a time of growing inequality and eroding social capital... The timing of the two trends is striking: somewhere around 1965–70 America reversed course and started becoming both less just economically and less well connected socially and politically."*

Viewed through Sapolsky's decades of scientific investigation into the physiology of stress, and backed by everything we've observed since the Great Decoupling in 1973 where national productivity has continued to grow but wage growth has been non-existent, it becomes disappointingly clear that all of this is actually of our own making. Through the policy decisions we've made to increase inequality in the blind pursuit of unlimited growth through the cutting of taxes and subsidizing of multi-national corporate interests, and through the pursuit of globalization without regard for its effects on the middle classes of developed nations such that 70% of households in 25 advanced economies saw their earnings drop in the past decade, we've created a societal feedback loop for chronic stress. And we're paying the price.

But it doesn't have to be this way. Just as we know more about why things are the way they are because of some rats in cages and some baboons in East Africa, those same animals point the way forward.

Creating Better Environments

In what was a sad day for Sapolsky but a remarkable day for science, he discovered back in the mid-1980's that the very first baboon troop he'd ever studied had experienced a die-off. Half of the troop's males had died of tuberculosis from eating tainted garbage. Because those at the top did not allow weaker males and any of the females to eat their prize trash, all of them died. The result was a truly transformed society of baboons.

Baboon Paradise

A greater sense of egalitarianism became the new rule of the jungle, so to speak. Bullying of females and lower males became a rarity, replaced with aggression limited to those of close social rank. Aggressive behaviors like biting were reduced while affectionate behaviors like mutual grooming were increased. The baboons got closer, literally. They sat closer to each other. Stress plummeted, even among those at the very bottom of the new hierarchy. Even more amazingly, this happier more peaceful society of baboons has lasted over the decades, despite members leaving and joining.

In what appears to be a transmission of societal values, new baboons are taught that in this particular society, bullying is not tolerated and tolerance is more the general rule, not the exception. Essentially, a new feedback loop was created, where the sudden reduction in inequality led to less stress and greater community, which led to a new normal of less stress and greater community. As Dr. Frans B. M. de Waal, the director of the Living Links Center at the Yerkes National Primate Research Center of Emory University put it in a 2004 interview with the *New York Times* about the baboon findings, "The good news for humans is that it looks like peaceful conditions, once established, can be maintained."

As much as the story of these baboons have to reveal about the importance and the hope of a less stressed-out, more peaceful society, there is another animal story that in my opinion shows the most potential for mankind of all.

[…]

Creating Human Park

It is only in my studies of the idea of basic income that I've seen glimpses into this idea of a Human Park. Like a bunch of puzzle pieces that can be collected to form into a picture, the evidence behind simply giving people money without strings forms a profound image of a better world that can exist right now, if we so choose. Remember the three primary factors that determine our levels of stress?

More Equality

Creating a less unequal society is step one. There exists in the world today, and has since 1982, something as close to a fully *universal* basic income as anything yet devised. It's the annual Alaska dividend where thanks to every resident receiving a check for on average around $1,000 per year for nothing but residing in Alaska, inequality is consistently among the lowest of all states. Not only that, but we see what we'd expect to see in lower stress populations, where Alaska is also consistently among the happiest states.

In Gallup's 2015 ranking of states by "well-being," Alaska was second only to Hawaii. This annual ranking is a combined measure of five separate rankings: purpose (liking what you do each day and being motivated to achieve your goals), social (having supportive relationships and love in your life), financial (managing your economic life to reduce stress and increase security), community (liking where you live, feeling safe and having pride in your community), and physical (having good health and enough energy to get things done daily). Alaska scored 5th, 5th, 1st, 7th, and 6th respectively in each of these measures.

In other words, in the only state in the U.S. to provide a minimum amount of income to all residents every year, such that no one ever need worry about having *nothing*, they feel the greatest amount of basic economic security and the least amount of stress than any other state. As a result they're also among the most motivated, the healthiest, and have strong family, friend, and community social supports. Alaska is essentially a glimpse at Human Park, but only a glimpse because even the $2,100 they all received in 2015 is not enough to cover a year's worth of basic human needs.

Improving Personality

Some more of the best evidence we have in the world for what happens in the long-term when people are provided something that looks even more like a basic income than is found in Alaska, can again be found in the U.S., in North Carolina.

In 1992, the Great Smoky Mountains Study of Youth began with the goal of studying the youth in North Carolina to determine the possible risk factors of developing emotional and behavioral disorders. Because Native Americans tend to be underrepresented in mental health research, researchers made the point of including 349 child members of the Eastern Band of the Cherokee Nation. About halfway into the ten-year study, something that is the dream of practically any researcher happened as a matter of pure serendipity. All tribal members began receiving a share of casino profits. By 2001 those dividends had grown to $6,000 per year. By 2006, they were $9,000 per year. The results were nothing short of incredible.

The number of Cherokee living in poverty declined by 50%. Behavioral problems declined by 40%. Crime rates decreased. High school graduation rates increased. Grades improved. Home environments were transformed. Drug and alcohol use declined. Additionally, the lower the age the children were freed of poverty, the greater the effects as they grew up, to the point the youngest ended up being a third less likely to develop substance abuse or psychiatric problems as teens. Randall Akee, an economist, later even calculated that the savings generated through all the societal improvements actually exceeded the amounts of the dividends themselves.

However, the most powerful finding of all was in personality effects. These changes were observed as a result of better home environments that involved less stress and better parental relationships. Incredibly, the children of families who began receiving what we can call something very close to a basic income, saw long-term enhancements in two key personality traits: conscientiousness and agreeableness. That is, they grew up to be more honest, more observant, more comfortable around other people, and more willing to work together with others. And because personalities tend to permanently set as adults, these are most likely lifelong changes.

If we remember how important personality is to the perception of stress and one's location within social hierarchies, these children will end up far better off, and as a result, their own children likely will as well. This is another glimpse into a basic income-enabled Human Park.

Increasing Social Cohesion

Although what's been happening for years in both Alaska and North Carolina are close to universal basic income in practice, they are not actually UBI. UBI requires regularly giving everyone in *an entire community* an amount of money *sufficient to cover their basic needs*. This has been done in three places so far: the city of Dauphin in Canada, the Otjivero-Omitara area of Namibia, and the Madhya Pradesh area of India.

It's in these areas that humanity has achieved what's closest to creating Human Parks. As a direct result of guaranteeing everyone a basic income in Dauphin, hospitalization rates decreased 8.5% and high school graduation rates surpassed 100% as dropouts actually returned to school to finish. In Namibia, overall crime rates were cut almost in half and self-employment rates tripled. In India, housing and nutrition improved, markets and businesses blossomed, and overall health and well-being reached new heights. But if it's one thing I find most interesting across all experiments, it's the improved social cohesion—a proliferation of new and strengthened social supports.

In Namibia, a stronger community spirit developed. Apparently, the need to ask each other for money was a barrier to normal human interaction. Once basic income made it so that no one needed to beg anymore, everyone felt more able to make friendly visits to each other, and speak more freely without being seen as wanting something in return. In India, where castes can still create artificial social divisions, those in villages given basic income actually began to gather across caste lines for mutual decision-making. And in Canada, the basic income guarantee had a notable impact on caring, with parents choosing to spend more time with their kids, and kids spending more time with each other in schools instead of jobs.

Remember, social supports are the trump card of societies with less stress, and it appears that providing people with UBI strengthens existing social supports and creates new ones. Freed from a focus on mere survival, humans reach out to each other. This is also something that makes us different from every other animal on Earth—our ability to reach each other in ways unimaginable even to ourselves until only recently. We as humans are entirely unique in our ability to belong to multiple hierarchies, and through the internet create connections across vast distances and even time itself through recorded knowledge.

Our place in a hierarchy matters, but we can decide which hierarchies matter more. Is it our position in the socioeconomic ladder? Is it our position in our place of employment? Or is it our position in our churches, our schools, our sports leagues, our online communities, or even our virtual communities within games like World of Warcraft and Second Life?

Reaching Our Potential

We as humans have incredible potential to create and form communities, and realize world-changing feats of imagination, and this mostly untapped potential mostly just requires less stress and more time. If all we're doing is just trying to get by, and our lives are becoming increasingly stressful, it becomes increasingly difficult to think and to connect with each other. It's the taxation of the human mind and social bonds. Studies even show the burden of poverty on the mind depletes the amount of mental bandwidth available for everything else to the tune of about 14 IQ points, or the loss of an entire night's sleep. Basically, scarcity begets scarcity.

On the other hand, if we free ourselves to focus on everything else other than survival, if we remove the limitations of highly unequal and impoverished environments, then we're increasingly able to connect with each other, and we minimize learned helplessness. As a result, our health improves. Crime is reduced. Self-motivation goes up. Teamwork overtakes dog-eat-dog, and long-term planning overtakes short-term thinking. Presumably, many an IQ *jumps* the equivalent of 14 points. A greater sense of security has even been shown to reduce bias against "out" groups, from immigrants to the obese. And if we take into account the importance of security in people deciding to invest their time and resources in bold new ventures, innovation also has the chance of skyrocketing in a society where everyone always has *enough* to feel comfortable in taking risks without fear of failure. Basically, abundance begets abundance.

If what we seek is a better environment for the thriving of humans—a "Human Park" full of greater health and happiness—then what we seek should be the implementation of basic income, in nation after nation, all over the world. There is no real feeling of control without the ability to say no. Because UBI is unconditional, it provides that lever to everyone for the first time in history. No other policy has the transformative potential of reducing anywhere near as much stress in society than the lifelong guaranteeing of basic economic security with a fully unconditional basic income. Plus, with that guarantee achieved, the fear of technological unemployment becomes the *goal* of technological unemployment. Why stress about automation, when we could embrace it?

No more fight-or-flight.

It's time for live long and prosper.

Poverty Is a Product of Underserved Neighborhoods

Anok

Blogger is a blog-publishing service that allows multi-user blogs with time-stamped entries. Anok has been a blogger since 2007.

A discussion over at BlogCatalog about affirmative action - turned socio-economic conditions debate has sparked my need to read. The question that sparked this exploratory post was whether not impoverished people could lift themselves up out of poverty by the very simple act of not making poor personal choices. At first, this question seems exceedingly simple to answer - better choices create better environments and results, therefore yes, making better personal choices would lift people out of poverty. Of course, the real answer is no where near that simple. In fact, the matter is so complex one could invest a lifetime exploring the causes and implications of poverty and socio-economic standing. I'm thinking we could do a brief overview, instead.

There are some common ideologies about poverty, crime, education and so forth that are often used in debates about the issue.

- Poverty is a choice, the poor choose to remain poor, the poor could lift themselves out of poverty by applying themselves, and the poor consciously make bad decisions to perpetuate poverty.
- The poor have no choices, are victims and are generally helpless.
- Poverty is caused by various means, and is a self perpetuating cycle that will require a concerted effort on everyone's behalf to break or correct.

Now, all of these ideologies have a bit of truth to them, but none of them are all true. First and foremost, we have to consider

"Is Poverty a Personal Choice?" by Anok, Blogger.com, November 20, 2008. Reprinted by permission.

our national economic system's role in poverty. We have a mixed economy that leans heavily towards free market capitalism. In capitalism economic hierarchies must exist, and be appropriately filled in order for capitalism to thrive. That includes the economic class of poor and working class economic brackets. Although extreme or abject poverty provides little benefit for regulated capitalist markets, those who hover right around the poverty threshold fulfill the basic needs of companies offering low wage employment. Students whose age and academic schedules determine that they work part time jobs, or fewer than twenty hours a week means that there simply aren't enough bodies to satisfy the needs of companies. So adults, particularly adults with little or no education, must step in and fill those positions.

Of course, we all know that supporting oneself or one's family on a low, minimum wage, or below minimum wage job (service industry, commission based jobs) is next to impossible, hence you have an entire segment of the population who are now poor. I find it ironic that the very requirements of an economic system that people support causes and sustains poverty, and yet, the poor are consistently blamed for their own financial woes.

Education Is Key

The most commonly looked at issue regarding poverty is education, or a lack thereof. Large cities with poor inner city schools are severely lacking in the funds and resources needed to provide decent, or competitive educations. To compound that issue, poor inner city areas also have little in the way of out-of-school educational resources, such as proper libraries, extracurricular activities, youth groups and organizations, tutoring and so forth. The children growing up in poor inner cities simply do not have access to all of the materials and information they need to become successful.

Drop out rates, rates of illiteracy, and poor educational resources result in poor test scores, low paying job opportunities, and a lack of value on education. Compare graduation statistics by cities and, Compare the test results of schools with high vs low levels of poor students. The numbers speak for themselves. However, even more pertinent to the problem are parents with equally low levels of education. Cognitive development studies have shown, over decades of research, that children with parents who have secondary, graduate, or post graduate educations will have children who develop faster and retain information better than children whose parents have little or no education, and for a variety of reasons.

Also, an interesting study and thesis points out that young adults with little to no education, or a poor education, living at or below the poverty level could adversely affect the unborn child and young child respectively due to a lack of pre-natal medical care, inability to properly parent, and exposure to insufficient role models and peer groups.

Essentially, the idea is that uneducated parents produce uneducated children, and instead of each generation experiencing a progression towards a decrease in poverty, the percentage of poverty and poor education actually increases.

Crime Doesn't Pay

Well, actually, it does pay. Crime pays well, in fact for a lot of people who would otherwise be scraping by a meager minimum wage and welfare living. There are a lot of arguments circulating around about the relation of poverty and crime. However, incarceration statistics clearly indicate that far more convicted criminals are coming from, and returning to, impoverished neighborhoods. There are anecdotal arguments about how not all poor people commit crimes, and never would, and that's true. However morals are relative and learned behaviors so it would suffice to say that those growing up who are exposed to crime, and have little education, and little hope for real opportunities have a much higher chance of committing a crime than those who do not grow up under those circumstances. A debate on the direct and indirect links of crime and poverty states:

Poverty creates unstable communities. Clifford R. Shaw and Henry D. McKay's classic 1942 study on juvenile delinquency argued that economic deprivation encourages crime only because poor neighborhoods tend to be socially unstable, [and] Unstable employment creates despair. More recent studies, however, have had to revise this aspect of the theory, the authors write. In his 1987 work The Truly Disadvantaged, William Julius Wilson showed that low-skill, high-paying manufacturing jobs in U.S. cities declined drastically during the 1970s. The result has been a concentration of poor blacks in ghetto areas. These areas have experienced extremely high rates of violent crime even though they are not subject to a job-driven turnover of population. [and] low levels of economic well-being directly encourage crime because people naturally shift to illegal activities in order to succeed when legal channels are blocked. [and] Obviously, deciding whether or not social disorganization mediates economic deprivation and crime depends crucially on how "social disorganization" and "economic deprivation" are defined and measured.

A look into the history of gangs and gang violence sheds even more light on the subject of crime, gangs, and violent crimes:

> The black youths in Aliso Village, a housing project in East Los Angeles, started a club called the Devil Hunters in response to the Spook Hunters and other white clubs that were engaging in violent confrontations with blacks. The term "Devil" reflected how blacks viewed racist whites and Ku Klux Klan members. The Devil Hunters and other black residents fought back against white violence with their own form of violence.

Although organized crime was nothing new at that time, the organization of gangs that evolved into what we know as the Bloods and Crips started for a very real, logical reason. *Protection and survival* from racist groups. These gangs, of course, evolved over time, and sought to use their power and numbers to create wealth in areas where poverty reigned supreme. I find it highly disingenuous to claim that poverty and an already violent environment had and has nothing to do with gangs and crime, considering that the gang members are often very, very poor. Top ten poverty locations and gangs. There is a psychology of poverty and social stigma attached to impoverished areas that when paired with an actual need to make money makes ganglife a desirable choice. Not only is the gang member making money to support himself or his family, he is also now commanding respect (through fear and violence) so that he gains power, social respect, and protection for himself, and his family members.

Although "gangbanging" is frowned upon by mainstream society, it garners a particular type of fear based respect from almost everyone. The moment you hear that someone is from a gang, be it the Bloods or the Hell's Angels, the reaction is immediate, and noticeable. One immediately knows not to challenge such a person, much in the way we would react to a brightly colored, venomous plant or animal. The genetic predisposition to stay away from that which endangers us is strong even in social circles. That kind of respect, although generally negative, still retains it's power. And when a person or group of people grow up feeling powerless, gaining social power and respect can and does become a priority. Crime pays out in this respect in a very big way.

It also helps to remember that the ideology of wealth being a desirable goal, and that the wealthy are notably respected for being able to acquire such wealth permeates every aspect of our society. It generates respect, awe, and power along with the financial ability to do whatever you please. This concept is not lost on those living in impoverished areas. In fact, I would say that living with the social stigma of poverty creates a huge desire to accumulate as much wealth as possible.

Look at it like this, if the temptation to commit a crime exists within wealthy, educated people so much so that they commit crimes to attain more wealth when they already have it, it's fair to say that those without educations, and no wealth to speak of, and no real possibility of attaining said wealth, the temptation to commit crimes to attain wealth increases accordingly. Although arguments of needs and wants may creep in, the psychological concept of *willingness* to commit a crime to accomplish the same goal remains unchanged, and would seem to be even more likely at lower levels of the economic structure, particularly when greed is combined with desperation.

Back to Education...

You might be saying to yourself, "But, but, but there are other ways to gain respect, and wealth than crime, we all know that!" And, to an extent, you would be thinking correctly. However, there are other forces at play here that when combined create the the right environment for crime. First and foremost, the lack of [quality] education immediately creates very real barriers to gainful employment above and beyond poverty wages. But you also have to address the psychological issues at play when poverty strikes or persists.

In the above argument about why crime and poverty are linked, it addresses unstable communities, and despair. This is important because when despair sets in, it works a bit like clinical depression, and may even be clinical depression. If a person has been living in poverty, struggling for their entire lives, or if a person has fallen into poverty with the inability to cope, they not only view the reality of severely limited choices as a large barrier, but may even refuse to accept a golden opportunity if one should come along. When you combine despair or depression, or even anger with a lack of education, or training for critical thinking you create a person who may not recognize, understand, or comprehend the available options, and may even create a fear of the unknown.

When you live among criminals and hustlers, you gain the street knowledge of healthy skepticism. If something is too good to be true, it probably is. With a life dedicated to scraping by a meager living, the thought of losing even more by way of a scam can be terribly frightening. Although I'm sure the temptation exists. In that regard, even a true opportunity may be interpreted as a scam.

Can anyone argue that these fight or flight reactions, the basic survival reactions ingrained in our genes are really *personal* choices?

They are choices, of course, but the idea that one is making a calm, educated choice with a future goal in mind in an impoverished and crime riddled environment with a lack of education is taking some creative license with the notion of "choice".

What Does It All Mean?

If we look at the Census Bureau's statistics on poverty we will see that 13% of the population lives at or below the poverty threshold, and 17.5% of the population hovers right above the threshold, or what is known as 125% of poverty. That would suggest that over 30% of the population is living at, below, or just above the national poverty threshold. That amounts to 91.5 million men, women, and children who are either in, or sinking into poverty.

We can argue that 30% of the population are simply making poor life choices, and leave it at freewill's doorstep, or we can address the very real issue of income and opportunity disparity in this country. 91 million people can't all be making the same simple mistakes. As we look at the history of gangs, the history of crime, the history of impoverished neighborhoods, and the history of the US we can get a general idea of what happened and why, where it all began. Unfortunately the task at hand now is breaking the violent cycle of poverty and crime. Knowing how it all began is a decent start, but doesn't speak to the changes we need to make it stop.

An answer lies somewhere, and it's time we really tried to find it.

The Myth of the Government-Provided Safety Net

Chris Velasco

Chris Velasco is Co-Founder and Executive Director of PLACE. PLACE is a nonprofit organization with a mission baked right into their acronymic name: Projects Linking Art, Community, and Environment.

Welcome to part four of PLACE's five-part series, *Talking About Poverty*. As our guide, we will be using the excellent series, *Busted: America's Poverty Myths* from WNYC's On the Media.

In our fourth part, we examine the myth of the safety net, which supposes that if any of our fellow Americans experience hard times, there are programs that, like a safety net, will catch them before they fall. We will also examine a recent quote from Speaker Paul Ryan in which he said, "We don't want to turn the safety net into a hammock that lulls able-bodied people to lives of dependency."

The corollary to the Myth of the Safety Net is that few of us need a safety net. Actually, the need is great, and the number of our neighbors living on the precipice is alarming.

Sixty-four percent of Americans don't have enough money to cover a $1,000 expense should it arise. In 2014, half of American households surveyed said they could not come up with $400 in an emergency. Half.

Between the ages of 25 and 60, nearly 40% of Americans will experience at least one year below the official poverty line. Yet, many leaders say that the safety net is too large and too luxurious, that we cannot afford it.

Take a look at GoFundMe, a site that allows people to help others in an emergency. You will see story after heartbreaking story of people who have suffered horrific fires, accidents and other tragedies. For them, there appears to be no other safety net than asking the internet for help.

What programs comprise our safety net? Let's start with the most basic of human needs, water.

When attempts to slash the government budget in Flint, Michigan resulted in poisoning of the water supply, what safety net was in place? The answer is none. An estimated 6,000 to 12,000 children were exposed to high levels of lead that will lead to long-term health consequences. Finally, after the crisis had dragged on for two years with no safety net in place, a judge finally ordered bottled water to be delivered. Recently, an investigation by Reuters has identified more than 3,300 areas with rates of childhood lead poisoning at least double those of Flint.

What about shelter? In 2017, a census-style count found 549,928 homeless people in America. And that number may be much higher, since the count did not include those people staying with a family member, a neighbor, or in their car. There are shelters, but almost all of them are private, not part of a public safety net.

The largest affordable housing program in America (Section 42) helps people who have the income to pay reduced rent. It is neither a program aimed at homelessness, nor is it a safety net. If you're homeless in America, there's nobody coming to help you.

How about the safety net for the sick? Even though the percentage of Americans without health insurance hit an all-time low in 2016, over twenty percent of Texans still had no coverage. While every other developed nation manages to provide health care for all its citizens, there is still no safety net for millions of sick Americans.

And then there is food. If you do not have anything to eat in America, there is a safety net. It's called the SNAP program (often known as food stamps) and it helps the poorest Americans, mostly children, and people who are elderly, disabled, or temporarily unemployed. The number of Americans seeking help from this safety net program was over 45 million in 2016.

However, SNAP was able to help only 85% of eligible individuals in 2013. This year, President Trump's "skinny budget" would slash the SNAP program by $150 billion over the next ten years, ending food assistance for millions of low-income families.

I wonder if anyone in the administration connected the moniker "skinny budget" with a 26% cut to the food stamps program. All safety net programs face severe cuts today under the "skinny budget." Other safety net programs to be cut include, Children's Health Insurance, Medicaid, Temporary Assistance to Needy Families, and—you get the picture.

Why are these social programs—underfunded to begin with—being cut further?

One reason is the perception that these programs do not work. The budget plan states, "Too many people are becoming trapped in the program with no way to get out. At the same time, states simply do not have the flexibility or authority to improve the program and address this cycle of dependency."

The reality is quite different.

Republican leaders have advocated that cutting benefits to poor people will motivate them to get a job and pull themselves up by their bootstraps (See Talking About Poverty Part 3), or put another way, the best way to help people is not to help people.

Pew, a nonpartisan organization, has analyzed the data and found:

- For people of all ages, the official poverty rate in the US was 14.5%. That's equivalent to 45.3 million people.
- Without food stamps, the poverty rate would be 17.10% – another 8 million Americans would be living in poverty.
- Without social security, the poverty rate for Americans 65 and older would be 52.67% instead of the current 14.6%. Without tax credits like the federal earned income tax credit, poverty for children under 18 would be 22.8% instead of the official poverty rate of 19.9%.

In other words, the data show the opposite. Cutting safety net programs plunges more people into poverty. Helping people helps people. Not every time. We all know an example of someone who can't seem to be helped. But those people are the exception. The lives of most poor people is a never-ending, fire-fighting crisis.

James Baldwin once wrote, "Anyone who has ever struggled with poverty knows how extremely expensive it is to be poor." Lower wage earners pay more for public transit because they can't afford a monthly pass. They rely on old cars that tend to break down and cost more to fix. They pay more for car insurance because of where they live.

If you earn less, you're less likely to eat healthy food because healthy food costs on average forty-five dollars more every month, and food costs more in poorer neighborhoods. You might not be able to afford the high fees for a bank account, and you cash your paycheck at places that take a huge cut. You also pay a higher percentage of your income in taxes than higher-income people. It's death by a thousand cuts.

And we're talking about adults. For kids, they are less likely to thrive when they suffer from poor nutrition, increased lead and environmental poisoning, growing up in stressful neighborhoods, inadequate medical care, and lack of access to good education.

The safety net has huge holes, too many to be a true net. The safety net is actually more of a ledge that some people might catch on the way down.

And it certainly isn't a hammock. My brother-in-law, is profoundly developmentally disabled, He cannot take care of himself. He receives just over $1,100 per month in benefits (much of it from Social Security benefits when his father died) to pay for housing, food, clothing and transportation in Minnesota. I am certain that Speaker Ryan does not refer to him, or the one-in-six American children born with developmental disabilities. I am certain he is not referring to our elders, who have worked their entire adult lives and now are retired on a fixed income that forces them to live in poverty. I am certain he also does not refer to people suffering from mental illness, caring for sick or dying loved ones, or the sick themselves, or disabled veterans.

Who, then, is left to be lying in a hammock, lulled into a life of dependency?

PLACE is a nonpartisan organization. We do not support candidates or political parties. But we can and do speak out on issues. On this issue of our safety net, Speaker Ryan is incorrect. The safety net is a myth and the hammock is an offensive stereotype.

When we create programs to help destitute people—a true safety net—the economy wins, the health care system wins, the educational system wins, and we can lower our spending on all these programs. We all win. Because as Senator Paul Wellstone once said, "We all do better when we all do better."

Part five of our series, Talking About Poverty, will discuss poverty and the media, the way America reports on poverty, and how it can shape your perceptions. We hope you will continue to send us your thoughts.

Organizations to Contact

The editors have compiled the following list of organizations concerned with the issues debated in this book. The descriptions are derived from materials provided by the organizations. All have publications or information available for interested readers. This list was compiled on the date of publication of the present volume; the information provided here may change. Be aware that many organizations take several weeks or longer to respond to inquiries, so allow as much time as possible.

Beyond Housing
6506 Wright Way
St. Louis, MO 63121
phone: (314) 533-0600
email: info@beyondhousing.org
website: www.beyondhousing.org

Beyond Housing helps communities become better places to live. They are a comprehensive community development organization convening partners and providing leadership. From purchasing a home to health, education, jobs, and economic development, they offer holistic resources and support.

Carpenter's Shelter
930 North Henry Street
Alexandria, VA 22314
phone: (703) 548-7500
email: information@carpentersshelter.org
website: http://carpentersshelter.org

Carpenter's Shelter supports the homeless to achieve sustainable independence through shelter, guidance, education, and advocacy. Carpenter's Shelter serves more than six hundred homeless and formerly homeless children and adults each year. Carpenter's comprehensive continuum of care offers continuous services, aiding the chronically homeless and shelter residents through their transition back into independent living.

Center for Community Change
1536 U Street NW
Washington, DC 20009
phone: (202) 339-9300
website: communitychange.org
email: info@communitychange.org

The Center for Community Change's mission is to build the power and capacity of low-income people, especially low-income people of color, to change their communities and public policies for the better.

The Coalition on Human Needs
1120 Connecticut Avenue NW
Suite 312
Washington, DC 20036
phone: (202) 223-2532
email: delliot@chn.org
website: www.chn.org
The Coalition on Human Needs (CHN) is an alliance of national organizations working together to promote public policies that address the needs of low-income and other vulnerable populations. The Coalition's members include civil rights, religious, labor, and professional organizations, service providers, and those concerned with the well being of children, women, the elderly, and people with disabilities.

Common Bond Communities
1080 Montreal Avenue
St. Paul, MN 55116
phone: (651) 291-1750
email: info@commonbond.org
website: commonbond.org

Common Bond Communities has provided homes and support for those most in need. Common Bond Communities was formed in 1971 with a goal of creating affordable housing during a time of significant racial and economic injustice. Today they provide homes and services for nearly twelve thousand people every year. They develop, own, or manage more than six thousand affordable rental apartments and townhomes throughout fifty-six cities in Minnesota, Wisconsin, and Iowa.

National Coalition for the Homeless

2201 P Street NW
Washington, DC 20037
phone: (202) 462-4822
email: info@nationalhomeless.org
website: http://nationalhomeless.org

The National Coalition for the Homeless is a national network of people who are currently experiencing or who have experienced homelessness, activists and advocates, community-based and faith-based service providers, and others committed to a single mission: to prevent and end homelessness while ensuring the immediate needs of those experiencing homelessness are met and their civil rights protected.

The Pew Charitable Trusts

One Commerce Square
2005 Market Street
Suite 2800
Philadelphia, PA 19103-7077
phone: (215) 575-9050
email: info@pewtrusts.org
website: www.pewtrusts.org

The Pew Charitable Trusts is driven by the power of knowledge to solve today's most challenging problems. They are an independent nonprofit organization. Pew applies a rigorous, analytical approach to improve public policy, inform the public, and invigorate civic life.

RESULTS
1101 15th St. NW, Suite 1200
Washington, DC 20005
phone: (202) 783-7100
email: results@results.org
website: www.results.org

Results is a movement of passionate, committed everyday people. Results is a nonprofit, grassroots advocacy 501(c)(4) organization that pushes for specific policies and legislation to address poverty. They empower people to become powerful voices for the end of poverty through grassroots advocacy.

Robin Hood
826 Broadway, 9th Floor
New York, NY 10003
phone: (212) 227-6601
email: info@robinhood.org
website: www.robinhood.org

Robin Hood reduces barriers to opportunities for nearly half a million New Yorkers. From keeping more than two hundred thousand New Yorkers from going hungry, to helping more than ten thousand of their neighbors secure jobs, to helping nearly eleven thousand remain stably housed and off the streets, Robin Hood is there for their neighbors. While Robin Hood's primary focus is on New York, their impact extends far beyond the borders of the city.

Southern Poverty Law Center
400 Washington Ave.
Montgomery, AL 36104
phone: (888) 414-7752
website: www.splcenter.org

The Southern Poverty Law Center (SPLC) is dedicated to fighting hate and bigotry and to seeking justice for the most vulnerable members of society. Using litigation, education, and other forms of advocacy, the SPLC works toward the day when the ideals of equal justice and equal opportunity will be a reality.

Stand Up For Kids

83 Walton Street NW, Suite 500
Atlanta, Georgia 30303
phone: 1 (800) 365-4543
email: staff@standupforkids.org
website: www.standupforkids.org

Stand Up For Kids is a nationally recognized nonprofit charity that works directly with thousands of homeless youth across the country. The organization was founded in 1990 by a group of volunteers in San Diego, CA. Starting as a program in one city, Stand Up For Kids has grown to sustain locations in eighteen cities across eleven states and the District of Columbia.

UnidosUS

1126 16th St. NW Suite 600
Washington, DC 20036
phone: (202) 785-1670
email: info@unidosus.org
website: www.unidosus.org

UnidosUS, formerly known as NCLR, has remained a trusted, nonpartisan voice for Latinos since 1968. They serve the Latino community through research, policy analysis, and state and national advocacy efforts, as well as in their program work in communities nationwide. They partner with a national network of nearly three hundred affiliates across the country to serve millions of Latinos in the areas of civic engagement, civil rights and immigration, education, workforce and the economy, health, and housing.

Warren Village
1323 Gilpin Street
Denver, CO 80218
phone: (303) 321-2345
email: info@warrenvillage.org
website: warrenvillage.org

Warren Village exists to help low-income single parent families achieve personal and economic self-sufficiency—and to sustain it. Single parents living at Warren Village are dedicated to improving their lives and creating a better future for their children and themselves. Warren Village has provided shelter to over 3,500 families since 1974 and has been a proud national model for its housing and programming structure including family services, early childhood education, and school-age programs.

Bibliography

Books

Anthony B. Atkinson. *Inequality*. Cambridge, MA: Harvard University Press, 2015.

Mehrsa Baradaran. *The Color of Money: Black Banks and the Racial Wealth Gap*. Cambridge, MA: Harvard University Press, 2017.

Keno Evol. *Let Me Live*. Binghamton, NY: Arissa Media Group, 2013.

Andrea Flynn, Susan R. Holmberg, Dorian T. Warren, and Felicia J. Wong. *The Hidden Rules of Race: Barriers to an Inclusive Economy*. New York, NY: Cambridge University Press, 2017.

Jeff Hobbs. *The Short and Tragic Life of Robert Peace*. New York, NY: Simon and Schuster, 2015.

Carolee Laine. *The War on Poverty*. Minneapolis, MN: ABDO, 2016.

Noël Merino. *Poverty and Homelessness*. New York, NY: Greenhaven Press, 2014.

Keith Payne. *The Broken Ladder: How Inequality Affects the Way We Think, Live, and Die*. New York, NY: Penguin, 2017.

Richard Rothstein. *The Color of Law: A Forgotten History of How Our Government Segregated America*. New York, NY: Liveright Publishing, 2017.

Robert S. Rycroft. *The Economics of Inequality, Discrimination, Poverty, and Mobility*. New York, NY: Routledge, 2017.

Martin E. P. Seligman. *Flourish: A Visionary New Understanding of Happiness and Well-Being*. New York, NY: Simon and Schuster, 2012.

Karen Steinman. *Poverty*. Broomall, PA: Mason Crest, 2017.

Bryan A. Stevenson. *Just Mercy*. New York, NY: Random House Children's Books, 2018.

Matt Taibbi. *The Divide: American Injustice in the Age of the Wealth Gap*. New York, NY: Random House Publishing Group, 2014.

Linda Tirado. *Hand to Mouth: Living in Bootstrap America*. New York, NY: Penguin, 2015.

Periodicals and Internet Sources

Emily Badger and Margot Sanger-Katz, "Who's Able-Bodied Anyway?" *New York Times*, Feb. 3, 2018. https://www.nytimes.com/2018/02/03/upshot/medicaid-able-bodied-poor-politics.html.

Reverend William Barber and Dr. Liz Theoharis, "America once fought a war against poverty – now it wages a war on the poor," *Guardian*, April 15, 2018. https://www.theguardian.com/commentisfree/2018/apr/15/poor-peoples-campaign-systemic-poverty-a-sin.

Jillian Bauer-Reese, "Reframing economic injustice in America's poorest big city," *Columbia Journalism Review*, May 11, 2018. https://www.cjr.org/united_states_project/broke-in-philly-poverty-journalism.php.

Charles M. Blow, "Poverty Is Not a State of Mind," *New York Times*, May 18, 2014. https://www.nytimes.com/2014/05/19/opinion/blow-poverty-is-not-a-state-of-mind.html.

Vanita Gupta and Fatima Goss Graves, "Medicaid work requirements are a throwback to rejected racial stereotypes," *USA Today*, January 11, 2018. https://www.usatoday.com/story/opinion/2018/01/11/medicaid-work-requirements-throwback-rejected-racial-stereotypes-gupta-graves-column/1024134001/.

B. Rose Kelly, "Sociology 207: Poverty in America course focuses on lived experiences of U.S. poor," Woodrow Wilson School of Public and International Affairs, April 16, 2018. https://www.princeton.edu/news/2018/04/16/poverty-america-course-focuses-lived-experiences-us-poor.

Craig Kielburger and Marc Kielburger, "Here's Scientific Proof That Poverty Can Be Inherited," *Huffington Post*, June 26, 2015. https://www.huffingtonpost.ca/craig-and-marc-kielburger/poverty-inherited_b_7663842.html.

Nicholas Kristof, "Is a Hard Life Inherited?" *New York Times*, Aug. 9, 2014. https://www.nytimes.com/2014/08/10/opinion/sunday/nicholas-kristof-is-a-hard-life-inherited.html.

Paul Solman, "Analysis: How poverty can drive down intelligence," *PBS News Hour*, May 11, 2018. https://www.pbs.org/newshour/economy/making-sense/analysis-how-poverty-can-drive-down-intelligence.

Samuel Stebbins, "Despite overall sustained GDP growth in US, some cities still hit hard by extreme poverty," *USA Today*, April 23, 2018. https://www.usatoday.com/story/money/economy/2018/04/23/cities-hit-hardest-extreme-poverty/528514002/.

Valerie Strauss, "Teacher: What I can't do for students," *Washington Post*, November 8, 2013. https://www.washingtonpost.com/news/answer-sheet/wp/2013/11/08/teacher-what-i-cant-do-for-students/.

Index